# SEEKING CHRIST

## A Christian Man's Guide to Personal Wholeness and Spiritual Maturity

### DR. DAVID STOOP

JANET THOMA BOOK

THOMAS NELSON PUBLISHERS
Nashville • Atlanta • London • Vancouver

Published in Nashville, Tennessee, by Thomas Nelson Inc., Publishers, and distributed in Canada by Word Communications, Ltd., Richmond, British Columbia.

Printed in the United States of America.
1 2 3 4 5 6 — 99 98 97 96 95 94

# Foreword

I was raised in a Christian home, and several times during my childhood I made commitments to Jesus Christ as my Savior. But I didn't really understand the nature of the choice I was making until I graduated from high school. That summer I attended a church camp. As I was sitting on the back row and listening to the speaker, the truth of the Good News challenged me. I was not eleven and deciding to make a little boy decision. Instead I was 18 and about ready to go off to college. I understood my decision and the meaning behind it. I decided to follow Christ. I mark my conversion from that point.

Like every new believer I immediately wanted to develop a close, personal relationship with Christ. And in the next two years, as I attended a Christian college, I read my Bible, memorized important Scriptures, and was exposed to wonderful Bible teachers who seemed to possess that close relationship to Christ. I talked with them at length to try to find any insight into what I needed to do to experience that closeness.

Then I took a position as a paid leader in an independent youth ministry. Part of what drew me to that position, as well as to the pastoral positions I held in the coming years, was the hope that somehow I would experience a particular closeness with the Lord because I was in ministry. Yet a massive piece of plexiglass seemed to be between me and Christ. I could see this relationship in others, but I couldn't make it mine. I didn't doubt my salvation, I simply couldn't feel my heavenly Father's presence.

Actually that same invisible wall had separated my earthly father from me. My dad had a hair-trigger Irish temper, and never openly expressed his love. He died when I was twenty-two, and after that I took what little I had known of him and tucked it safely away in my memory. At the same time I put him on a pedestal and idealized him.

I remember thinking, *When my first son is born, I will do this fathering thing differently. I will get close to my kids.* Twenty years later I became totally frustrated with myself as I realized that I had repeated the same pattern with my sons. And despite my years of searching for closeness with God, that relationship was still a mirror image of my relationship with my own dad.

In the next years I tried to better understand my dad and how he had shaped me. As I did so I started to realize my own struggles to be a man and a father in today's world. And that plexiglass wall between the Lord and I also began to disintegrate.

Over the years since that time, I have talked with a number of men who have had the same experience. They viewed God through the reflection of their relationship with their dads. If dad was a tyrant, so was God. If dad was distant or absent, so was God. If dad was unforgiving, so was God. If dad couldn't be trusted, neither could God. By understanding the patterns of their pasts, they were able to break free into their own manhood—and to find satisfaction and fulfillment in seeking Christ.

As I made my journey to find a closer relationship with the Lord I answered certain questions and noted those answers in a journal. That process helped me to better visualize my relationship with my dad and the Lord. For this reason I have designed a new type of devotional: a Pen & Ink devotional, which allows you to note your reflections about how the passage relates to you and your everyday life. These devotions have a Scripture passage and a meditation on that passage, and then reflections and a prayer. Also, study questions from each week are included in the final pages of the book. These are ideal for a small men's Bible study or prayer group. I'd encourage you to begin the process of growth in your own life and find a small group of men to work through these issues.

I pray that in the next sixteen weeks, as you meditate on these Pen & Ink devotionals, that plexiglass barrier between you and your dad and between you and the Lord will be removed for you, as it was for me.

# SEEKING
# CHRIST

# Consider the Rock

**What was your father like?**

_____

_____

_____

**What kind of relationship did you have with him?**

_____

_____

_____

> **I**n looking back, we do not have to be afraid to look at both the good and the bad.

ISAIAH 51:1–3
*"Listen to Me, you who follow after righteousness,
You who seek the LORD:
Look to the rock from which you were hewn,
And to the hole of the pit from which you were dug.
Look to Abraham your father,
And to Sarah who bore you;
For I called him alone,
And blessed him and increased him."
For the LORD will comfort Zion,
He will comfort all her waste places;
He will make her wilderness like Eden,
And her desert like the garden of the LORD;
Joy and gladness will be found in it,
Thanksgiving and the voice of melody.*

**H**ow many times, as you were growing up, did you hear someone say, "You're a chip off the old block"? Or how many times did someone tell your dad, "You son's just like you. He's a chip off the old block?" As I was growing up, people told me that I was tall and skinny like my dad. I bore some resemblance to him. In many ways, all of us are "chips off the old block." That's why Isaiah said to Israel, "Look to Abraham your father, and to Sarah who bore you. . . ." We can only understand some important things about ourselves by looking back at our childhood and those who raised us. As men, we especially need to look at our fathers.

You are about to begin a journey towards greater wholeness as a man. Deep inside, every man hungers for greater righteousness, for knowing God more intimately, and for understanding more of what it means to be a man in today's world.

Yet some of us are afraid to truly look at our past. Yes, we will look back to explain the good we see in ourselves or others. "He is like that because his father taught him well," we might say. And we would be telling the truth. But to say the opposite—"He is struggling because his father failed him"—becomes uncomfortable, perhaps even unthinkable. We want to praise the good and deny the existence of the bad. Yet both are true.

Think about Abraham. The good is obvious: He left his own country to wander in the wilderness at God's command. In fact, throughout his life his faith in God was so deep he is called the spiritual father of all Christians. But the bad is just as true: Abraham stretched the truth. In fact, he lied. He said that his beautiful wife, Sarai, was his sister so the rulers of these foreign lands would not kill him to marry his lovely wife. Abraham was not perfect. Neither are our dads today. And some of us are struggling because of the way our fathers treated us.

Perhaps that's why Isaiah says it is so important to "Look to the rock from which you were hewn." Then, to make certain the Israelites understood his point, he repeated the thought more directly: "Look to Abraham your father." The promise Isaiah gave them, and gives us, is that by doing so we will find joy and gladness. Take a moment now to think about your dad. Look at both the good and the bad—and try to accept them both.

*Lord, help me to see my dad as he truly was and to understand that he is different from my heavenly Father who is perfect in His love for me.* ■

**REFLECT**

In what ways are you a chip off the old block?

_____

_____

_____

**REFLECT**

Describe something good that your father instilled in you.

_____

_____

_____

"**A guaranteed way to repeat the past is to ignore it.**"

# Remember Your Roots

**REFLECT**

How do you resemble your father in looks and in personality?

_____

_____

_____

**REFLECT**

What are some of the things you missed in your relationship with your dad? Describe several of them.

_____

_____

_____

> **M**emories of your father can be a well-spring of knowledge, wisdom, and heritage on which you may draw.

DEUTERONOMY 32:7–9

*"Remember the days of old, consider the years of many generations.*

*Ask your father, and he will show you; your elders, and they will tell you:*

*When the Most High divided their inheritance to the nations, when He separated the sons of Adam, He set the boundaries of the peoples according to the number of the children of Israel.*

*For the LORD's portion is His people; Jacob is the place of His inheritance."*

**S**ome of us treasure something that belonged to our father, even though it may be worthless to someone else. I've got a red Shaffer mechanical pencil from my father. In a desk drawer, it just looks like any other mechanical pencil. To me it is a treasure because of what I can remember from it. When I was just beginning to write at age six, my dad purchased a red Shaffer pencil for me. Being a kid, I promptly lost it. A couple of years later, I understood the importance of the pencil. I saved my money and managed to buy another one for dad. After he died, it is one of his few personal items that I have. It is a family heirloom and my way of remembering that relationship.

We remember at other times too. One stage of development in life is called the "crisis of generativity," the time when, as adults, we look at what we have contributed to life, either in terms of our work or of our children. Then we ask, "Will I leave something behind? Will I be remembered?" This yearning is universal. It was true in Bible times—and it's just as true today. In 2 Samuel 18:18, Absalom set up a monument for himself because he did not have a son to carry on his name. Today magnates like Donald Trump build buildings and name them after themselves: Trump Tower, Trump Plaza, Trump Park, Trump Palace, Trump Castle, Trump Airlines. It is important to be remembered. And it is equally important to remember.

Yesterday, Isaiah told us to look to our roots and remember. Today, we see Moses telling the people to "Remember the days of old. . . . Ask your father, and he will show you." For more than forty years, Moses led the nation of Israel. Now in his final days of life, Moses called the nation to assemble together. He wanted to remind them of the stories in their past but to do it in a familiar way. Moses recited the words of a song. Throughout his leadership, Moses had seen the people rebel and grumble. He knew it was even more likely that they would stumble after his death. The song that Moses told would be a continual witness to the people.

When you were a child, your father built some values into your life. Possibly your father taught you the importance of telling the truth. Or through trial and error you learned the difference between right and wrong. For a moment, consider those memories of your father during your growing-up years. Memories are a gift. Maybe you have an old pocketknife or an engraved watch. What kind of treasure do you have? That family treasure evokes some precious memories about your father.

What were some of the ways your father hurt or disappointed you as you were growing up?

_____

_____

_____

What are the things you vowed would be different when you had sons and daughters?

_____

_____

In what ways did you fail to make this happen?

_____

_____

_____

*Memories are sometimes deep in my mind, Lord. Bring them to the surface so I can understand the values that my father has built into my life.* ■

**"Will I leave something behind? Will I be remembered? This yearning is universal."**

# *Abraham's Dilemma*

**REFLECT**

Were there any events in your growing-up years that you didn't understand, and maybe still don't understand? Describe them.

_____

_____

_____

**REFLECT**

What are some of the things that weren't discussed in your family?

_____

_____

_____

> **W**e're usually taught to bottle up our emotions inside, but how often do we consider the consequences of our silence?

GENESIS 22:10–12

*And Abraham stretched out his hand and took the knife to slay his son.*

*But the Angel of the LORD called to him from heaven and said, "Abraham, Abraham!" So he said, "Here I am."*

*And He said, "Do not lay your hand on the lad, or do anything to him; for now I know that you fear God, since you have not withheld your son, your only son, from Me."*

**T**alk about an experience to remember! Abraham and Isaac would never have forgotten this event. And they might never have fully understood God's request.

Abraham thought he knew what God had asked him to do. What do you think went through his mind as he and his son Isaac, along with two other young men, rode silently for three long days to Mount Moriah to make a sacrifice—without an animal to sacrifice? There is no question that Abraham loved his son, Isaac. He was 100 years old before he and Sarai had a child, and then they named him "Isaac," *laughter* because of their joy and the impossibility of their becoming parents at this age. How could Abraham make it through those three days, knowing that his precious son was to be the sacrifice?

Think of the questions that must have raced through Abraham's mind, all the doubts about what he had heard God say to him. These doubts and concerns must have confronted Abraham with each step he took. We know the end of the story, but for almost four days and three nights, Abraham didn't know what God had in mind.

And what about Isaac? He must have questioned as well. Finally, as they began to climb the mountain,

Isaac asked what he had been wondering all along: Where is the lamb? Where is the sacrifice we are to offer? His father did not really give him an answer. As Isaac was tied up and placed on the wooden altar, what terror went through his young mind as he realized he was to be the sacrifice? Did Abraham look at him as he took the knife in his hand?

Logically, the event does not make sense. And emotionally, there is no way to understand it either. Soren Kierkegaard wrote a short treatise on this biblical event entitled *Fear and Trembling*. He said, "I would first depict the pain of his trial. To that end I would, like a leech, suck all the dread and distress and torture out of a father's suffering, so that I might describe what Abraham suffered, whereas all the while he nevertheless believed."

Some might say that Abraham and Isaac never discussed what happened on Mount Moriah because men in that culture didn't talk about things like that. Neither do many of us today. That's not really the "manly" thing to do. We're usually taught to bottle up our emotions inside—to "tough it out." But how often do we, or did Abraham, consider the consequences of our silence? The impact of that silence—ours or our own father's—can be devastating.

Whether our silence about hurtful things is part of our culture, or simply due to our fearfulness to confront one another, the consequences are the same as when we remain silent about our hurts—we end up distanced from the people we love, and from God Himself.

*God, help me to be open with my children, especially with my sons, so that I can give them the gift of open and honest communication.* ∎

**REFLECT**

Why do you think it was so hard to talk about those kinds of things?

_____

_____

_____

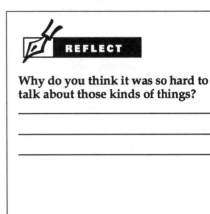

**REFLECT**

Who were you able to talk to?

_____

_____

_____

"**When we as men bury our hurts and misunderstandings, silence in our relationships is often the result.**"

# *A Question of Love*

**What are some of the hurtful things that weren't discussed in your family?**

_____

_____

_____

**Some families only acknowledge the goodness within them. When we are raised in this type of situation, there is often a lot of pressure on the children to live up to the family. The children in these homes often have difficulty in finding their own niches in life. What sorts of expectations within your family were difficult to live up to?**

_____

_____

_____

> **W**hen we fail to talk about our hurts, we end up distanced from the people we love, and from God Himself.

PROVERBS 27:1–6

*Do not boast about tomorrow,*
*For you do not know what a day may bring forth.*
*Let another man praise you, and not your own mouth;*
*A stranger, and not your own lips.*
*A stone is heavy and sand is weighty,*
*But a fool's wrath is heavier than both of them.*
*Wrath is cruel and anger a torrent,*
*But who is able to stand before jealousy?*
*Open rebuke is better*
*Than love carefully concealed.*
*Faithful are the wounds of a friend,*
*But the kisses of an enemy are deceitful.*

**D**eath. Illness. Lost jobs. Broken relationships. As we look at the suffering and reality of hurt and evil in the world around us, many of us struggle with being able to believe and trust in a living God. Our faith is put to the test and we struggle to keep our faith.

After that journey to Mt. Moriah, what happened to the faith of Isaac? Unfortunately, it appears that he never quite recovered from this traumatic experience. As happens with many of us, Isaac appears to have withdrawn into silence about God.

If you read through the Genesis stories and consider Isaac and his two sons, you'll discover that his sons knew little about this incredible God. Isaac seldom spoke of matters of faith. He withdrew into silence about God and it created a distance between men for over three generations. Unfortunately this distancing is all too common in our own experience as well. My father and I had a similar type of relationship. Dad never talked much about his faith in Jesus Christ. Instead, he took me to church and figured that I would get my spiritual teaching there. His lack of involvement in my spiritual teaching created a distance between our relationship. My relationship with my dad was a microcosm of my relationship with my Heavenly Father. The distance with my dad cut down on my intimacy with God, the Father.

As a counselor and pastor, I know that many men have experienced the same sort of distance. When we fail to talk about our hurts and the faith-stretching parts of our lives, we end up distanced from the people that we love, and from God Himself. In the *wisdom* literature of the Bible, we learn the importance of breaking our silence. Part of an ageless principle is that "open rebuke is better than love carefully concealed."

Do you long to narrow the distance between you and your dad? The first step may be talking about your hurts. As we are open about our hurts, we gain the support and love of those around us. We break down the barriers that separate us as men from others and look a bit more human.

Showing your hurts isn't easy. Remember that the things we don't talk about in our families are given more power to repeat themselves by our silence. Even taking some initial steps to talk about it can lower some barriers. It may be the first step toward a lasting relationship with your father and heavenly Father.

**REFLECT**

Are there some things that you vowed would be different when you had a family?

_____

_____

_____

**REFLECT**

How can you break the pattern of silence? List some specific steps.

_____

_____

_____

"**Open rebuke is better than love carefully concealed.**"

*Lord, help me to begin to lower the barriers I've created so I can talk about my faith with my dad and my children.* ∎

# *Secrets*

**REFLECT**

What secrets did you share with your father growing up?

_____

_____

_____

**REFLECT**

What secrets did you want to share with your dad but could not share with him?

_____

_____

_____

> **G**od wants us to share our secrets with Him— that's one of the reasons that we pray.

GENESIS 24:61–67
*Then Rebekah and her maids arose, and they rode on the camels and followed the man. So the servant took Rebekah and departed.*

*Now Isaac came from the way of Beer Lahai Roi, for he dwelt in the South.*

*And Isaac went out to meditate in the field in the evening; and he lifted his eyes and looked, and there, the camels were coming.*

*Then Rebekah lifted her eyes, and when she saw Isaac she dismounted from her camel; for she had said to the servant, "Who is this man walking in the field to meet us?" And the servant said, "It is my master." So she took a veil and covered herself.*

*And the servant told Isaac all the things that he had done.*

*Then Isaac brought her into his mother Sarah's tent; and he took Rebekah and she became his wife, and he loved her. So Isaac was comforted after his mother's death.*

**A**fter Isaac's mother died, Abraham found a wife for Isaac. The Bible passage for today says that when he married Rebekah, he "was comforted after his mother's death." It's too bad that father and son couldn't comfort each other. Instead it took another woman.

Imagine both of these two grown men grieving over the death of Sarah. But neither one allowed the other to know the depth of their pain. It was like some great secret that couldn't be made known. In *Peculiar Treasures*, Frederick Buechner wrote that "I not only have my secrets, I am my secrets, and you are your secrets." Through sharing these secrets with another human, we can unlock ourselves. Then we can learn what it is to be human. In fact, that's when we can begin to discover more of what it means to be a man.

Buechner added, "I am inclined to belive that God's chief purpose in giving us memory is to enable us to go back in time so that . . . we can have another go at it." I don't think either Isaac or Abraham ever forgot about that morning on Mount Moriah. But since they didn't talk about the secrets of their hearts concerning that episode, they lost a part of themselves as well as isolated themselves from each other.

Perhaps part of Abraham's trial on the mountain was not only whether or not he would obey God, but also whether he could be open with his son about what he and God were doing. We need to remember that Abraham was a man—just like us. Through his obedience, his faith was confirmed and on that point he was successful. But through the silence of the days that followed, his relationship with his son grew more and more distant. And on that point, he failed.

Many of us have shut down. We don't even open up in our relationship with God. We figure the Lord knows, so why talk it over with Him. Yes, God does know everything, but because He honors and respects our personhood, He respects our secrets. He wants us to share them with Him—that's one of the reasons that we pray. Through the graciousness of God, He never says to us, "I already knew all of that."

**REFLECT**

Are there some secrets that you still keep that you have never shared? List three.

_____

_____

_____

*God, trust is something that comes with practice. Help me to deepen my trust in You today and share with You some of the secrets from my heart.* ∎

**"Sharing our secrets with one we trust is not only part of becoming known, it is part of knowing ourselves."**

# Openness vs. Strength

**When have you told someone else, such as your parents, about your hurts? Describe the situation.**

_____

_____

_____

**Often a pattern weaves itself through our hurts over the years. Can you see a pattern of being hurt in the same way, only by different people and in different settings? Describe the pattern.**

_____

_____

_____

> **R**elationships are always built on knowing each other's heart.

PSALM 139:14–16
_I will praise You, for I am fearfully and wonderfully made;_
_Marvelous are Your works,_
_And that my soul knows very well._
_My frame was not hidden from You,_
_When I was made in secret,_
_And skillfully wrought in the lowest parts of the earth._
_Your eyes saw my substance, being yet unformed._
_And in Your book they all were written,_
_The days fashioned for me,_
_When as yet there were none of them._

**O**ne of my friends was a risk-taker. If you asked him for his opinion, he always gave it. If you needed an idea for a project, this friend had plenty. Unfortunately, this friend was almost too open in expressing his ideas. He had thrown caution to the wind. After several months, his boss decided that he was too far out in front and no one was following his leadership. His job was terminated.

As men, we've been trained not to let anyone know our real opinions. In the workplace, when someone turns to us and says, "What do you think?" we've learned to be cautious in what we say. If we tell too much about ourselves, then it can be used against us. It makes us too vulnerable and that is just plain scary—especially to us as men.

When I talk about openness, I don't mean discussing the latest baseball scores or my golf handicap—those surface things are easy to talk about. When we talk about the weather or the headlines from the newspaper, there is no risk to the situation.

In the opening verses of Psalm 139, David invited God to search within him, and to know his heart. He was taking those initial steps to know himself and to know God. Besides learning more about God, David wanted a mutual relationship where he was also known by God. Relationship is always built on knowing each other's heart.

When I move beyond head knowledge and facts about the weather and sports and instead talk about my feelings, I risk a deeper part of myself to someone else. If you are the first one to risk sharing this type of information, it takes great courage. What if the other person laughs or doesn't understand? The response is unpredictable when you talk about feelings. But my experience has been that, if I risk sharing myself with someone else, then others will respond in kind. I can learn about the hurts and inner feelings of the other person. Our conversation moves toward an intimacy that can't be reached in just the facts.

King David showed his strength of character and courage through his willingness to risk before the Lord. I can risk talking about my areas of "woundedness" with others. My risk will not always be honored with openness from the other person. Sometimes, he or she may have a bit of embarrassment and quickly change the subject. But for me to grow as a person and learn to know the heart of others, it begins with a single step.

*Lord, give me the courage to risk moving my relationships to a deeper level.* ■

**REFLECT**

Did your father ever talk with you about his hurts? Do you remember times when you knew he was hurt, but was unwilling to talk?

_____

_____

_____

**REFLECT**

List some of the men who know about your woundedness or some men with whom you might be able to share some of your hurts.

_____

_____

_____

" **Only as we let others get to know us by sharing our hurts can we begin to know ourselves.** "

# Not My Family!

**REFLECT**

How was the family in which you were raised dysfunctional or sinful?

_____

_____

_____

**REFLECT**

Think about your family and your children. Describe some situations where you have been dysfunctional.

_____

_____

_____

> **W**e can only appreciate the goodness of our families when we acknowledge the problems.

GENESIS 25:21–26, 28

*Now Isaac pleaded with the LORD for his wife, because she was barren; and the LORD granted his plea, and Rebekah his wife conceived. But the children struggled together within her; and she said, "If all is well, why am I this way?" So she went to inquire of the LORD.*

*And the LORD said to her: "Two nations are in your womb, two peoples shall be separated from your body; one people shall be stronger than the other, and the older shall serve the younger." So when her days were fulfilled for her to give birth, indeed there were twins in her womb.*

*And the first came out red. He was like a hairy garment all over; so they called his name Esau. Afterward his brother came out, and his hand took hold of Esau's heel; so his name was called Jacob. Isaac was sixty years old when she bore them.*

*. . . And Isaac loved Esau because he ate of his game, but Rebekah loved Jacob.*

**W**hen we think of what families should be like, our first inclination is to believe that Abraham's family had it all together. But today's selection from Genesis gives us a very realistic picture of Abraham's family over a period of four generations. We discover that through the generations, Abraham's family had its problems. His family was as dysfunctional as anyone's.

Now you may balk at that word *dysfunctional*, for it is overused. But basically it is a synonym for *sinful*. According to the Bible, everyone is sinful. Therefore everyone, to some degree, is dysfunctional. And that includes my family as well as yours, and it even includes Abraham's family.

As we look at Abraham's family over the generations, there are several recurring problems and patterns. For one thing, both Abraham and Isaac lied, saying that their wives were really their sisters. Each man was afraid of being killed by someone who wanted to take his wife. A more obvious dysfunctional pattern in these families is where parents played favorites with their children, and we will look at this favoritism and the disastrous results next week.

Yet in spite of all the hurt and dysfunction within these families, God still chose to identify Himself in the Old Testament as the "God of Abraham, Isaac, and Jacob," those sinful, hurtful, dysfunctional people. God wasn't surprised by their behavior. He still loved them. In that caring action, He shows us that He is willing to meet us in the place where we have been hurt the most. He won't violate the boundaries of our secrets—it's up to us to let Him, and others we trust, into those places in our hearts.

Sometimes we are afraid to look at those hurts because we feel it will destroy the goodness we had in our families. The truth is, we can only appreciate the goodness when we acknowledge the problems. That's the way reality is—a blending of both good and bad. And our confidence is that God meets us in both places.

**REFLECT**

List some concrete steps that you will take to correct your sinful actions in the family.

_____

_____

_____

"**The truth sets us free; facing the truth about our families sets us free from the patterns of generations.**"

*Lord, help me to honestly look at my parents and my immediate family— with both the good and the bad. Use the insight to set me free.* ■

# *Troubled Manhood*

**REFLECT**

In what ways are you like your mother?

_____

_____

_____

**REFLECT**

List some ways you are different from your mother.

_____

_____

_____

GENESIS 26:6–11
*"So Isaac dwelt in Gerar. And the men of the place asked him about his wife. And he said, "She is my sister"; for he was afraid to say, "She is my wife," because he thought, "lest the men of the place should kill me for Rebekah, because she is beautiful to behold."*

*Now it came to pass, when he had been there a long time, that Abimelech king of the Philistines looked through a window, and saw, and there was Isaac, showing endearment to Rebekah his wife.*

*Then Abimelech called Isaac and said, "Quite obviously she is your wife; so how could you say, 'She is my sister'?" And Isaac said to him, "Because I said, 'Lest I die on account of her.'"*

*And Abimelech said, "What is this you have done to us? One of the people might soon have lain with your wife, and you would have brought guilt on us."*

*So Abimelech charged all his people, saying, "He who touches this man or his wife shall surely be put to death."*

**H**ave you ever seen an athlete look into the TV camera and say, "Hi, Dad"? I haven't. They all say, "Hi, Mom." It seems so natural. I've seen the same kind of thing happen when I ask a group of men to talk about their fathers. Usually there is an awkward silence, then the men struggle to describe their fathers, or say something about the relationship. But if I ask that same group of men to talk about their mothers, the conversation comes alive. And why not? Mom was always there for us while Dad was away working.

We've already noted that Isaac was probably closer to his mom than to his dad. When Sarah died, he grieved, and it was only through his marriage that he was comforted. When Abraham died, Isaac buried his father and went on with his life. So isn't that natural? Although most of

> **O**ur fathers help us develop a confidence from within for facing the challenges and dangers of life.

us have a similar experience to Isaac we also experience a deep hunger for a relationship with our father.

In *Fathers and Sons*, Gordon Dalby quotes clergyman Prentice Tipton: "When mothers lead the family because the fathers fail to lead—either by absenting themselves from the home or by taking a passive role—boys are deprived of the most important natural model of manliness. Growing up mainly under the supervision of women, many of them experience insecurity over their identity as men."

One of the important tasks for a father is to help us as men develop a confidence from within for facing the challenges and dangers of life. Without that help, on the surface we may appear to handle the situations well. But inside we have a gnawing fear that we work very hard to keep hidden from other people. This basic fearfulness led Isaac to lie about his wife, like his father had done before he was born, "'She is my sister,' ... because he thought, 'lest the men of the place should kill me for Rebekah, because she is beautiful to behold.'" It's interesting to note how the sin of Abraham is repeated in his son's life—even though he may never have known that his father did the same thing.

Also, fearfulness separated Isaac from his own sons. He had little time for Jacob. What time he did share with Esau was focused on doing, not on relating. Isaac remained unknown to his sons, just as his father had probably been unknown to him, except as a "giant of faith before his God." Like many of us, he also probably knew his father through his relationship with his mother. To be a man in today's world, we need to conquer this fear of the unknown and learn from other men who know what it means to be masculine.

*Lord, give me the strength for today as I relate to my father and my children. Help me to be open and break down any barriers.* ∎

**REFLECT**

Describe your relationship with your mother.

_____

_____

_____

**REFLECT**

How can you begin to take some concrete steps to conquer the fear of your relationship with your dad? With your children? Take one of them today.

_____

_____

_____

"**We can only know the Father by knowing our manhood.**"

# Turning Our Hearts

**REFLECT**

As you think about your father, how would you rate your relationship on a scale of one to ten in terms of closeness? Describe a moment of time when you were close.

_____

_____

_____

**D**uring the last days, dramatic change will take place in the father and children relationships.

MALACHI 4:1–6

*"For behold, the day is coming, burning like an oven, and all the proud, yes, all who do wickedly will be stubble. And the day which is coming shall burn them up," says the LORD of hosts, "That will leave them neither root nor branch.*

*. . . But to you who fear My name The Sun of Righteousness shall arise with healing in His wings; and you shall go out and grow fat like stall-fed calves. You shall trample the wicked, for they shall be ashes under the soles of your feet on the day that I do this," says the LORD of hosts.*

*"Remember the Law of Moses, My servant, which I commanded him in Horeb for all Israel, with the statutes and judgments.*

*"Behold, I will send you Elijah the prophet before the coming of the great and dreadful day of the LORD. And he will turn the hearts of the fathers to the children, and the hearts of the children to their fathers, lest I come and strike the earth with a curse."*

**M**y friend John has a father who vanished from his life at an early age because his dad was older. John's father never learned how to be a father—how to hold a good conversation or play catch out in the backyard. Whenever John tried to strike up a conversation with his dad, his dad just trivialized the attempt and quickly changed the subject.

Now John is an adult and has children of his own. He would still like to have a relationship with his dad. Part of John is afraid to push his father because of his father's age.

As I think about John's interaction with his father, it reminds me how much I enjoy watching a good action movie. Most of these movies are pretty predictable—the bad guy always gets caught in the end and is either eliminated or thrown into jail. There is something satisfying inside to know from the beginning how the movie will turn out.

Sometimes I wish real life was as simple and predictable. Unfortunately, some fathers disappear from their children's lives at a young age. These children spend a lifetime longing to know their dads. Other fathers meet a tragic death through an accident and their children never know them. In countless others, divorce has separated the father-son relationship.

In today's passage from Malachi, I take great comfort in what will transpire during the last days. It's better than a celluloid movie because the promise comes from the Eternal Father.

During the last days, dramatic change will take place in the father and children relationships. Fathers will turn their hearts to their children and the children will unite their hearts with the fathers. Such a reunion has been in God's plan since the beginning of time. We each know that something needs to change, for we all long for more from our fathers. God cares about that longing and wants to bring healing in those places where needed, and bring greater closeness for others.

The changes to make that reunion happen aren't easy. No one knows when the last days will come. But each of us have today to grow in our relationship with our parents.

*God, give me the means to develop closeness in my life—with my father, my children, or a friend.* ■

**REFLECT**

A relationship of closeness takes time to develop. How can you begin to develop this relationship with your father today? Can you make a phone call, write a letter, or give some other means of encouragement? Make a note of something specific.

_____

_____

**REFLECT**

Possibly your father isn't in your life because of death, divorce, or some other reason. Are there other men in your life with whom you can develop a close relationship? How can you begin today?

_____

_____

"**God longs to bring healing in those places where we need it.**"

# *Father of the Fatherless*

## REFLECT

Looking back, how would you describe your father's role in your life during your childhood?

_____

_____

_____

## REFLECT

When you were young, which of your characteristics did you sense that your father valued?

_____

_____

_____

> **W**e need to examine our fears and inadequacies about parenting and learn to have a greater impact in our families.

GENESIS 27:11–17

*And Jacob said to Rebekah his mother, "Look, Esau my brother is a hairy man, and I am a smooth-skinned man. Perhaps my father will feel me, and I shall seem to be a deceiver to him; and I shall bring a curse on myself and not a blessing."*

*But his mother said to him, "Let your curse be on me, my son; only obey my voice, and go, get them for me." And he went and got them and brought them to his mother, and his mother made savory food, such as his father loved.*

*Then Rebekah took the choice clothes of her elder son Esau, which were with her in the house, and put them on Jacob her younger son. And she put the skins of the kids of the goats on his hands and on the smooth part of his neck. Then she gave the savory food and the bread, which she had prepared, into the hand of her son Jacob.*

**O**ften manhood is seen as attending to the great affairs of the world and the family, but staying pretty much uninvolved in the direct parenting of our children. We leave that to their mothers. It's not that we don't love our children. All too often we are have some fears and inadequacies about parenting on a daily basis.

Isaac was raised by a father who cared, but might have been too busy to talk about some of the incredible things that went on in their relationships. Perhaps Isaac taught hunting to Esau. But his other son Jacob was abandoned to Rebekah, his mother.

Which situation creates greater problems for us as men: the abandonment of a father, or the busyness of a father that allowed him to only relate to us around his own interests? It's probably academic because in each case, Dad is absent in any meaningful way. At best, he only valued us for what we did, seldom for who we were.

Jacob might have been emotionally abandoned by Isaac and had a smothering relationship with his mother. This relationship led Jacob to develop a way of life that manipulated situations for his own advantage. In *Peculiar Treasures*, Frederick Beuchner makes the point that Genesis spells it out quite clearly—Jacob was a crook. Twice he cheated his brother out of what was rightfully his. At least once he deceived his own father to steal his brother's birthright, then conned his father-in-law Laban out of his flocks and became a very rich man in the process.

God has promised to be a father of the fatherless, and the Lord parents in a beautiful way. Notice that when God and Jacob finally got to meet (see Genesis 28:10–17), God didn't take advantage of the situation and begin trying to straighten up Jacob's crooked life. Instead, God started out gradually and introduced Himself to Jacob. Then the Lord told Jacob how He was going to bless him. That's the kind of father we all long for—one who loves us and accepts us for who we are. That's grace. And that type of grace is what our fathers are supposed to demonstrate to us. If our dads fail, then God fills in the gap himself!

**REFLECT**

**What characteristics or values do you wish your father had seen in you, but did not?**

_____

_____

_____

**REFLECT**

**If you have children, how would they describe your presence in their day to day lives?**

_____

_____

_____

> "**Some things can be gotten through manipulation, but other things can only be given through love.**"

*Sometimes when I look at spending time with my children, Lord, I find it frightening. Help me to face those fears and inadequacies and increase my role as a father.* ∎

# Man's Work

**REFLECT**

What were some of the things you were taught by your mother about what it means to be a man?

_____

_____

_____

**REFLECT**

What are some of the ways these ideas have made it more difficult for you as a father or a husband or a man today?

_____

_____

_____

> **If our father is absent, our mom tries to fill the void but her concepts of manliness may be inadequate.**

GENESIS 29:15–20
*Then Laban said to Jacob, "Because you are my relative, should you therefore serve me for nothing? Tell me, what should your wages be?"*

*Now Laban had two daughters: the name of the elder was Leah, and the name of the younger was Rachel. Leah's eyes were delicate, but Rachel was beautiful of form and appearance.*

*Now Jacob loved Rachel; and he said, "I will serve you seven years for Rachel your younger daughter."*

*And Laban said, "It is better that I give her to you than that I should give her to another man. Stay with me."*

*So Jacob served seven years for Rachel, and they seemed but a few days to him because of the love he had for her.*

My dad worked long hours as a spot welder while I was growing up. He left home early in the morning and came home tired. It was as though a sign was tattooed across his forehead—I'm unavailable. It was late in life at the age of thirty-five that my dad married. So he was older and well-established in his life-long habits before I came into his life. Learning the proper means to father wasn't a part of my dad's experience; my grandfather died when my dad was a teenager.

As I can say from personal experience, when Dad isn't around much, Mom fills the void. That's to her credit, but it doesn't provide for us the understanding of what it means to be a man. Mom is the taxi driver to run the kids to their sports games or karate lessons. Then, when the older children have homework, Mom spends hours helping them get their assignments finished on time. Some of the mothers that I know have even taken an active interest in sports. After school, these moms toss a ball in the backyard with their sons—a task that is traditionally given to fathers.

It almost sounds contradictory that a woman—Mom—should teach a young man what it means to be a man in today's world. That's a job for Dad. That's not to fault Mom, but this is "man's work."

Earlier this week, we've been reading about Jacob and how his mother, Rebekah, taught him that if he wanted to get ahead in life, he should manipulate others. Apparently, Rebekah was teaching her son what she had learned about men during her growing-up years. As she watched her father and uncles, deception was commonplace and a way of life. This family trait is evident in Rebekah's brother Laban. He tricked Jacob into marrying his older daughter, Leah, before Jacob married Rachel. Deception was woven into the family lifestyle. Jacob learned his conning methods from his mother.

No matter how hard she works at filling a void left by an absent dad, Mom usually relies on cultural definitions of manliness, or what she was taught in her family by her father. Because of the many cultural misconceptions about manliness, she usually compounds the problems instead of fixing them.

Absentee fathers are prolific in this country. That's why social agencies like "Big Brothers" are so helpful, particularly in the inner cities. The disappearing father perpetuates the problem of men understanding their maleness instead of solving it. The solution is for fathers to take a more active role in the lives of their children.

*Lord, teach me what it means to be a man in today's world. Bring people into my life today that can help me.* ■

**REFLECT**

Can you think of situations where you still feel like a little boy around other men?

_____

_____

_____

**REFLECT**

Describe some of the ways you cover up this "little-boy" feeling?

_____

_____

_____

> **"Growing up on the outside isn't enough; we need to grow up on the inside as well."**

# *Sins of the Fathers*

**REFLECT**

Name the destructive patterns in your family and describe how they affected you as you grew up. Was lying condoned, for instance? Favoritism?

_____

_____

_____

**REFLECT**

How have these patterns affected you as an adult?

_____

_____

_____

**D**etermine today to be the transitional person in your family tree.

GENESIS 37:3–5, 11
*Now Israel loved Joseph more than all his children, because he was the son of his old age. Also he made him a tunic of many colors.*

*But when his brothers saw that their father loved him more than all his brothers, they hated him and could not speak peaceably to him.*

*Now Joseph dreamed a dream, and he told it to his brothers; and they hated him even more. . . .*

*And his brothers envied him, but his father kept the matter in mind.*

**A**s we've continued reading about Abraham's family, we notice that the favoritism, which was played out over three generations, didn't improve over the years. Instead, it became more and more destructive to the individuals involved. What started out as Sarah's jealousy became Esau's thoughts of murder, and then these thoughts almost became murder from Joseph's brothers.

I don't believe Isaac or Jacob intentionally carried on this "family tradition" through the generations. They were simply acting out the principle that the "iniquity" of the fathers would be visited on the children over the generations. (See Exodus 20:5.) This is a principle that goes beyond sin or iniquity. The patterns within a family are continued from generation to generation—until someone becomes the "transitional person" in that family and brings about change.

It's reasonable to believe that both Isaac and Jacob were determined to be the one who stopped the destructive pattern in their families. I can imagine Isaac saying to himself when he learned that Rebekah was pregnant, *I'm going to be a different kind of father than my dad! There will be no favoritism in my family.* But then his circumstances were different—his wife had twins. And when Rebekah decided to align herself with Jacob, Isaac filled in the gap to some degree with Esau. Each parent had their favorite child and the pattern continued.

I'm certain that Jacob thought about the destructive pattern of playing favorites—possibly while he was traveling to his Uncle Laban's home. Jacob wasn't excited about moving to a strange part of the world. His life had been quite comfortable at home, especially the way his mother took such good care of him. As he walked through the wilderness on his first trip away from home, he could have thought to himself, *When I have a family, it's going to be different! I won't allow any favoritism!*

Of course, when he married, his circumstances were different. He ended up with two wives, but he only wanted to enjoy Rachel—the wife he really loved. Eventually the pattern of favoritism played out with his two wives; Jacob made a favorite of his son Joseph. Obviously, it is easier to say things will be different than to actually make things different.

That's true for us as well. Family influences run deep and often play themselves out in ways that we never could imagine. Eventually, the reality of what we have done hits us square in the face, and we realize we have repeated the pattern. There is a way out—we can change the patterns, but only when we are willing to face the pattern directly and develop a determined plan to change it.

*For me to change my old habits is not easy, Lord. I need You every hour to make a difference in my family.* ∎

**How have you repeated them as you have grown older?**

_____

_____

_____

**What would it take to begin to break the pattern?**

_____

_____

_____

> "**There is a way out—we can change the patterns.**"

# Leaving Home

**REFLECT**

To what degree have you left home emotionally? (One way to answer this question is to ask your wife, or a friend, how old you acted the last time you were with your parents. Or describe how old you felt inside when you were last with them.)

_____

_____

_____

**REFLECT**

What are some of the things you might lose if you were to leave home emotionally? (Sometimes it is financial support, or a sense of belonging somewhere.) What might you gain?

_____

_____

_____

> **The real task of growing up is more than physical. It means to leave home emotionally.**

PSALM 105:1–4
*Oh, give thanks to the LORD!*
*Call upon His name;*
*Make known His deeds among the peoples.*
*Sing to Him, sing psalms to Him;*
*Talk of all His wondrous works.*
*Glory in His holy name;*
*Let the hearts of those rejoice who seek the LORD.*
*Seek the LORD and His strength;*
*Seek His face evermore.*

Sometimes it's pretty easy for me to be skeptical about people. As a counselor, I see people in my office who repeatedly make the same mistakes. They are stuck in the same behavior as their parents and even their grandparents. Maybe they come from an alcoholic background. As children, they saw the destructive influence of alcohol on their fathers. Over and over, they watched their mothers cover up for the drunken nights and the missed meetings. But as they've grown into adulthood, these same people are almost magically drawn toward the same behavior to cope with their day to day problems.

Or maybe you watched your dad work long hours as a child. Sunday afternoons were about the only time that he was available to you. And even then he was so exhausted that he usually curled up on the couch and took a long nap. "I'll never be like that," you vowed. "I'll have more time and energy for my children." Yet as an adult, the call to work almost whispers in your ear and, like a lightening bug to an electric light, you are drawn to work extra hours.

One of my friends says that people never change. Lately, I'm beginning to agree with him, but with one important additional thought. "Yes," I said to him recently, "people don't change, but they can grow." Of course, as we grow—or in some cases, as we continue to grow up—we do change. Our task is to continue this growing-up process. Thankfully, as Christians we don't have to face this task alone; we can do it with God's help. As the Psalmist says in today's reading, we should seek the Lord and His strength.

A big part of growing up is leaving our parents. That may sound drastic, or traumatic, and in some cases it does feel that way. But the idea is to leave so that we can come back and relate to them as adults, not as children any longer. Other cultures have elaborate rituals to symbolize a boy's move into manhood. In some ways, it's unfortunate that we don't have anything so clear-cut. Through the ceremony, these boys change their relationship with adults. They are treated as adults instead of children.

Many of us moved out of our parents' homes and figured that that was our ritual. It meant that we were grown up. But the real task of growing up is more than moving out. It means to leave home emotionally. That's more difficult.

 **REFLECT**

Sometimes we fail to jump in with both feet, leaving one foot in the old place and the other foot in the new place. Often it is because we still want something—like approval—from our parents. What are some of the things you still want from your father? From your mother?

_____

_____

_____

 **REFLECT**

Take each thing you described in the last question and rate the probability of ever getting that from either parent.

_____

_____

_____

*Lord, You know I left my home physically. Now give me Your strength to leave home emotionally.* ∎

**"Part of letting go of the past means we will need to grieve what we will never get."**

# *What Is a Man?*

## REFLECT

Take some time and reflect on the four areas in your own life (physical, mental, spiritual, and social). If you were to list them in order of the time that you devote to them, what would the order be?

According to time

1. _____

2. _____

3. _____

4. _____

If you listed them in order of your success in each, what would the order be?

According to success

1. _____

2. _____

3. _____

4. _____

> **B**alance is essential as we grow into manhood.

LUKE 2:48–52

*So when they saw Him, they were amazed; and His mother said to Him, "Son, why have You done this to us? Look, Your father and I have sought You anxiously."*

*And He said to them, "Why is it that you sought Me? Did you not know that I must be about My Father's business?"*

*But they did not understand the statement which He spoke to them.*

*Then He went down with them and came to Nazareth, and was subject to them, but His mother kept all these things in her heart.*

*And Jesus increased in wisdom and stature, and in favor with God and men.*

**W**hat is a man? How do you answer that question? Do you look to some of the folk heroes of our age, like John Wayne, Alan Alda, or Norman Schwarzkopf? Do you look to some business success and define manhood through a Ted Turner or Ross Perot? Or do you turn to a more religious figure that defines manhood through a Billy Graham or Chuck Colson?

Part of our journey to manhood is to determine what we mean by manhood. First think about your own definition. Pause for a minute and determine the name of a person who typifies manhood for you. Then write down your own *current* definition. There is no right or wrong answer—let's simply explore some of our own presuppositions.

One way to approach the topic of manhood is to look at the God/Man, Jesus Christ. Often as we picture Jesus in our minds, we draw from the cultural emphasis about Christ—which places an emphasis on His meekness and mild manners. Pictures like Salmon's head of Christ give us a gentle version of Him. Other images of Jesus show Him with children or sitting in a boat on the edge of the Sea of Galilee teaching the people.

But other aspects of Jesus' manhood are found in the Gospels. In John 2, He picked up a whip and drove the merchants from the temple. The temple guards approached Jesus carefully and asked Him what authority He had to do what He did (See John 2:13–25.) In fact, all through the first half of John's Gospel, Jesus took on the power structure of Judaism, fearlessly standing up to the leaders. Even in Jesus' final day, Pontius Pilate was impressed by the inner authority He possessed. Certainly he saw another side of Jesus than the meek and mild picture.

Part of the true definition of manhood is based on what Luke says in verse 52: "Jesus increased in wisdom and stature, and in favor with God and men." There is a sense of balance in the growth of Jesus Christ. This balance included the physical, the mental, the spiritual, and the social—all areas we need within us in order to grow into manhood.

 **REFLECT**

**How would your family rate them for you?**

**According to family**

1. _____
2. _____
3. _____
4. _____

**"In what ways does your family of origin still set your priorities?"**

*Lord, search my heart and show me where I'm out of balance in my life.* ∎

# *The Impostor*

**REFLECT**

What authority issues are still unresolved between you and your father?

_____

_____

_____

**REFLECT**

What steps can you take to settle these authority issues?

_____

_____

_____

> **U**nresolved authority issues from our past will always affect our present, limiting our effectiveness as God's men.

1 SAMUEL 10:21–24

*When he [Samuel] had caused the tribe of Benjamin to come near by their families, the family of Matri was chosen. And Saul the son of Kish was chosen. But when they sought him, he could not be found. Therefore they inquired of the LORD further, "Has the man come here yet?" And the LORD answered, "There he is, hidden among the equipment."*

*So they ran and brought him from there; and when he stood among the people, he was taller than any of the people from his shoulders upward.*

*And Samuel said to all the people, "Do you see him whom the LORD has chosen, that there is no one like him among all the people?" So all the people shouted and said, "Long live the king!"*

**M**any of us look at the reign of King Saul and conclude, "Too bad. Either God made a mistake in picking Saul or He wanted to teach the Israelites a lesson for wanting a king." Both of these conclusions are weak: first, God doesn't make mistakes. And as far as the second one is concerned, why then did God pick David to be Saul's successor? Israel hadn't learned anything from Saul. A more reasonable explanation has to be that King Saul somehow failed at his task. (See chapters 11–12.)

Saul was a remarkable young man. In chapter 9, he is described as "a choice and handsome young man," who was also taller than anyone else. He was smart and compassionate. When he was acting in the strength of the Lord, he was a dynamic leader. So what went wrong?

There are several clues, one of which is in the Scripture verse for today. He apparently was very shy. When Saul was to be anointed as king—something he already knew was going to take place—he hid in the baggage area of the camp. He was a reluctant leader!

Now shyness is obviously not a sin. But shyness is related to fear, and it is difficult for someone to be a leader and to be dominated by fear. His fears seemed to be connected to his relationship with his father (see chapter 9).

According to tradition, Saul's father was a military leader and came from a family of strong, powerful men. While looking for his father's donkeys, Saul had a growing fear that his father would be worried. The servant with Saul was even more concerned about the father's potential displeasure if they failed to find the donkeys. So the servant urged Saul to continue his search. Both saw Saul's father as a man of great authority.

Apparently Saul never settled this authority issue with his father. Throughout his life, he struggled with authority. Saul struggled in his relationship with Samuel, who was an authority figure to him—even though Samuel had passed on the leadership to Saul. Following his early successes, Saul struggled with his own authority, giving in to the old fears again in the face of Goliath. And then, in the event that led to his downfall, Saul gave in fearfully to his troops and disobeyed God's instructions regarding the battle with the Amalekites (see chapter 15). One might say that Saul had an "impostor's complex." He never felt on the inside that he belonged in the position of king.

Like Saul, many men struggle today with the same complex, fearing that people around them will see through the facade to the fearfulness just below the surface. They are successful on the outside, but filled with fears on the inside.

*Today I've been able to name and face some of my fears. Use that process to make me more genuine to those around me.* ■

REFLECT

Discuss some of the ways you have been limited or controlled by your fears. What have been some of the consequences?

_____

_____

_____

REFLECT

In what ways have your fears led you to be controlled by others, even your parents, as you seek to gain their approval or keep them from thinking poorly of you?

_____

_____

_____

"**Many a man fears that people will see through his facade to the fearfulness just below the surface.**"

# *Fear Concealed*

**REFLECT**

Describe a time when you fear that you are an impostor who lives one life on the outside, but feels quite different on the inside.

_____

_____

_____

**REFLECT**

What things you have done to cover up your fears?

_____

_____

_____

_____

> **A**s we resolve the authority issues in our life, God's authority becomes much more comfortable to us.

**1 SAMUEL 15:22–26**
*Then Samuel said: "Has the LORD as great delight in burnt offerings and sacrifices, as in obeying the voice of the LORD? Behold, to obey is better than sacrifice, and to heed than the fat of rams. For rebellion is as the sin of witchcraft, and stubbornness is as iniquity and idolatry. Because you have rejected the word of the LORD, He has also rejected you from being king."*

*Then Saul said to Samuel, "I have sinned, for I have transgressed the commandment of the LORD and your words, because I feared the people and obeyed their voice. Now therefore, please pardon my sin, and return with me, that I may worship the LORD."*

*But Samuel said to Saul, "I will not return with you, for you have rejected the word of the LORD, and the LORD has rejected you from being king over Israel."*

**A**s a young associate pastor, I remember sitting in the monthly meetings of the church board. Forty-eight men and women gathered in the fellowship hall. The senior pastor conducted the meeting so I didn't have to participate much in the meetings—good thing because I was petrified to be there.

Although I didn't say anything about it and looked completely normal, I had a deep sense that I didn't belong in those meetings—they were for grown-ups and I had yet to break out of my little boy mold. I sealed my lips and kept them shut.

In the Bible section for today, Saul looked completely normal too—on the surface. In chapter 15 of 1 Samuel, Saul is rejected as king of Israel. As the first king of Israel, Saul stood taller than others around him. He was handsome and oozed self-confidence. But God told the prophet Samuel that Saul had failed as a king, because he disobeyed God's directions. When the Israelites conquered the enemy, God told them to totally destroy their enemies—all of the people and every animal. Instead, Saul went his own direction and brought back animals for sacrifice. His disobedience cost Saul the kingdom.

As I look around at the men in my life, many of them are like Saul. Some men worry about the outward appearances while they are struggling to stay alive on the inside. You may have the same struggle or have known that struggle at some point in your life. If you don't have fears in your current reality, often they seem to be lying there just beneath the surface.

Eventually, Saul's fears led him to lose everything. Fear has a way of doing that, especially when we try to ignore the causes. Some fears can be faced and overcome; others go deeper, giving us a feeling of powerlessness. When we try to ignore these fears, they often prove to be our undoing.

**REFLECT**

**Think about your struggles with authority. In what ways are your fears related to authority issues in your life? Do you have trouble accepting outside authority or accepting your own authority?**

_____

_____

_____

" **Some men worry about the outward appearances while they are struggling to stay alive on the inside.** "

*Lord, I want to move beyond outward appearances and consider who I am on the inside. Give me the wisdom to see and understand it.* ∎

# Out of Control

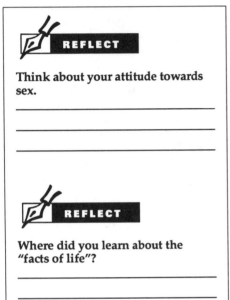

> **S**exuality is important, but it is not everything.

2 SAMUEL 13:12–14
*And she [Tamar the daughter of David] answered him [Amnon, the son of David], "No, my brother, do not force me, for no such thing should be done in Israel. . . .*
*. . . Now therefore, please speak to the king; for he will not withhold me from you."*
*However, he would not heed her voice; and being stronger than she, he forced her and lay with her.*

**W**hen a child is born, the doctor checks the genitals. Then depending on what he sees, the doctor announces whether the baby is a boy or a girl. Today, doctors are making the statement about the sex of the child even before birth. The doctor bases his announcement on what he or she sees on the ultrasound. When our dog has puppies, we look at the same place to determine their sex. Obviously, there has always been a physiological difference between men and women.

In *The Masculine Journey*, Robert Hicks notes that one of the Hebrew words for man is *zakar*, which literally means, "to be sharp, or pointed." This word refers directly to the male penis or phallus.

Remember the first time that you had to define yourself as a man? For most of us, it happens early in adolescence in a locker room. We defined ourselves as a man through our sexuality. Some men never get beyond this stage, and for them, sexuality becomes an idol.

All through the Bible, God sets limits on the expression of our sexuality. Some have looked at this and said that God is repressive. On the contrary, unless as men we can learn to balance the physical part of our masculinity with the other parts of our manhood, we will get ourselves in trouble and hurt those we love. Amnon is a perfect example of someone who was out of balance.

Amnon had no control over his sexual appetite. He fell in love with his half-sister, Tamar, and became "so distressed over his sister Tamar that he became sick." Tamar was a virgin, and Amnon knew that it was improper for him to have sex with her. But one day, perhaps in the locker room, Amnon and a friend made a plan so he could seduce Tamar. When he did, she resisted. Under the control of his passions, Amnon ignored reason and raped her. And afterwards? Tamar, the object of Amnon's love, became someone that Amnon hated. This happens so often when sex becomes our idol. What we first loved and once possessed becomes despised.

There are always consequences to unbridled sexuality. In this case, Tamar's brother Absalom became her avenger. For two years he waited and watched, and then his men murdered Amnon. Tamar's sexual violation was avenged, but at a great cost—Absalom had to flee for his life. Then Absalom was separated from his father, King David. Finally the consequences led to Absalom's death.

Amnon acted as if he were above the rules. His out-of-control sexuality became his idol, and he was never satisfied. The phallic male can never be satisfied, for his sexuality is not in perspective with the other aspects of manhood. Sexuality is important, but it is not everything. And if it seems as if it is everything, we need to look at how and why we have stopped developing into a balanced man.

*God, I want to have a healthy, balanced attitude about my own sexuality, but I can't do it on my own. Please help me.* ∎

**REFLECT**

How strong is your fantasy life? Do you struggle with it daily? Less often? More often?

_____

_____

_____

**REFLECT**

What have you found helpful in keeping your fantasy life on track?

_____

_____

_____

"**My attitude towards my sexuality is a good indicator of my growth and balance as a man.**"

# The "No Response" Response

**REFLECT**

How balanced is your sexuality with the other aspects of your manhood? Describe the position that sex holds in your priorities.

_____

_____

_____

**REFLECT**

If you are married, or if you have been married, where would your wife say sex is in your priorities? Is her view different, and why?

_____

_____

_____

> **D**avid was angry but didn't take any action against Amnon. He chose to respond with no response.

2 SAMUEL 13:19–22

*Then Tamar put ashes on her head, and tore her robe of many colors that was on her, and laid her hand on her head and went away crying bitterly.*

*And Absalom her brother said to her, "Has Amnon your brother been with you? But now hold your peace, my sister. He is your brother; do not take this thing to heart." So Tamar remained desolate in her brother Absalom's house.*

*But when King David heard of all these things, he was very angry.*

*And Absalom spoke to his brother Amnon neither good nor bad. For Absalom hated Amnon, because he had forced his sister Tamar.*

**T**hroughout the life of King David, one theme is consistent. In the tragic events related to his family, he was a passive father. Even when one of his children raped another of his children, David didn't take any action against Amnon. He was angry but chose to respond to the situation with no response.

Generally, David was not a passive man. The well-known stories about David show him as a man of action. But in this situation within his own palace, he acted passively and his troubles compounded.

Part of Absalom's anger following the rape of his sister was David's lack of response to either Tamar and Amnon. Amnon should have been punished, for he not only violated his family through his incest, he violated God's laws as well. But David did nothing.

For two years, his son Absalom waited to see if David would respond. Then Absalom took matters into his own hands. His men murdered Amnon and Absalom fled into exile for three years. During those years that Absalom was in exile, "David mourned for his son every day" (2 Sam. 13:37). When Absalom returned to Jerusalem, his father said it would be under one condition—that Absalom not see or speak to his father. How tragic! But the even greater tragedy is that David's pattern is not new. It continues today. Many of us had a similarly passive father. Underneath, our fathers probably want to have a active roles in our lives. Instead of moving ahead with courage, sometimes our fathers don't advance into unknown territory. Instead, they often delegate their responsibilities to our mothers—or to no one.

For example, one of my friends has a son who has reached the age at which he needs to have a frank discussion about sex. "My husband and I have talked this over," June admits to me. "But when he was growing up, his dad never talked about sex so he doesn't see why he needs to." In many ways, this man is a confident businessman, but when it comes to accepting his position as a father, he acts like a little kid. He doesn't have the confidence or courage to carry out his fatherly obligations and joys. Through our passivity, we have not acted with courage and compassion toward our sons and taught them how to be men. The generational pattern of destruction continues.

**REFLECT**

How much of your fantasy life is related to sex? What do you think you avoid by fantasizing about sex?

_____

_____

_____

**REFLECT**

Sometimes our problems in the sexual area are simply related to our inability to relate to women. Sometimes, like Samson in the Bible, we become easy marks to be manipulated by an unscrupulous woman. In what ways are you "weak" when it comes to relating to women?

_____

_____

_____

*Lord, I don't want to lead my family as a passive person; help me to take an active and balanced approach.* ■

"**Balance includes the idea of not taking sex too seriously, except to seriously keep it under God's control.**"

# Nowhere to Hide

**REFLECT**

When have you rebelled and done the exact opposite of what was best?

_____

_____

_____

**REFLECT**

In what ways are you running away (physically, emotionally or spiritually)? Describe them below.

_____

_____

_____

> **I**nstead of running away, we need to acknowledge our need of God's grace.

JONAH 1: 1–3

_Now the word of the LORD came to Jonah the son of Amittai, saying,_

_"Arise, go to Nineveh, that great city, and cry out against it; for their wickedness has come up before Me."_

_But Jonah arose to flee to Tarshish from the presence of the LORD. He went down to Joppa, and found a ship going to Tarshish; so he paid the fare, and went down into it, to go with them to Tarshish from the presence of the LORD._

**A**lmost everyone knows the story of Jonah and how he was swallowed by a "great fish." But the story of Jonah also tells of a man who turned and ran away from God.

We don't know Jonah's reason. Perhaps he was struggling to maintain his image. Nineveh was one of the enemies of Israel and he didn't want to look like a traitor. That's a reasonable concern for any self-respecting man. Or so it seemed to be. Rather than warn the enemy of coming destruction, Jonah thought that he should let God destroy them—the people in Nineveh deserved every bit of what they were going to get.

But in my view, the point of the story is that God told Jonah to go, and Jonah thought he could hide from God. How foolish! There is no place to hide from God, not even hell! (See Psalm 139:7–12.) But Jonah's running away is really not that different from many of our situations. Today, there seems to be an epidemic of men choosing to "run away" from all kinds of things. We run away from responsibilities, relationships, difficulties, and just about anything else that might expose us as being less of a man than we are trying to be.

We spend a lot of energy hiding from God, then acting as if the Lord couldn't possibly know. From early childhood, we are taught to hide. Some of us cover up better than others. We learned to swallow our hurt or disappointment, or else we would "really get something to cry over." We learned to brush off our knee and say "I'm okay" so our friends wouldn't think we were weak. In fact, according to a number of studies, this tendency to hide our feelings is a major reason that men do not live as long as women.

Hiding information and relationships amounts to great complexity in our lives. Sometimes the hiding gets so difficult, we just run away from facing it. We run away to work, or we run away to some addictive behavior, or we literally run away from those we love. We run because we don't know how we would survive if they knew us as we really are.

Jonah was good at hiding, even from himself. While the storm raged to the point of panic for the seasoned mariners, Jonah slept in the bottom of the boat. Then, once he was awakened, he silently watched as the sailors cast lots to see which one of them caused the problem. He didn't even volunteer to jump into the sea; instead he waited to be thrown in.

Only when Jonah had almost reached the literal end of himself did he change his attitude and open himself to what God wanted to do in and through him in the first place. Swallowed alive, sitting inside a great fish, near death, Jonah cried out for God's mercy. And in the graciousness of God, the Lord heard him and responded. For each of us, it takes acknowledging our emptiness and limitedness to find God's fullness and unlimited grace and mercy. The simple admission is the first step.

*Lord, I'm tired of running. I want to honestly face tomorrow and quit hiding. The only way it will happen is through Your life in me.* ∎

**REFLECT**

As you think about these hidden areas, what will it take to be more open about these situations? List them below.

_____

_____

_____

**REFLECT**

Many men feel that they are alone with their problems. How can you break out of the tendency to shut people out of the vulnerable and hurting parts of your life?

_____

_____

_____

"**Many of us have haven't found God's mercy because we haven't reached the end of ourselves. Instead, we've chosen to go it alone.**"

# *Running to Mercy*

Describe some ways you have "run away" over the years. Are there situations you once ran from that you can now face?

_____

_____

_____

What are some of the things you said you would never do, but ended up doing?

_____

_____

_____

> **F**ear and failure are only terminal when we give up.

LUKE 22:59–62

*. . . Another confidently affirmed, saying, "Surely this fellow also was with Him, for he is a Galilean."*

*But Peter said, "Man, I do not know what you are saying!" And immediately, while he was still speaking, the rooster crowed.*

*And the Lord turned and looked at Peter. And Peter remembered the word of the Lord, how He had said to him, "Before the rooster crows, you will deny Me three times."*

*Then Peter went out and wept bitterly.*

**N**ot everyone is a Jonah who runs away physically to escape a situation. We can run away in other ways. Peter ran away by simply denying his relationship with Jesus. Was he ashamed to be known as a friend of Jesus? Was he afraid for his life? Was he disillusioned by Jesus' arrest? Perhaps he simply denied the Lord out of fear.

During those final hours before his arrest, Jesus told Peter that he had prayed for Peter's faith not to fail. In boldness, Peter said that he was prepared to go to prison or even death. Then Jesus predicted that Peter would deny Him three times before the day was over.

*No way,* Peter probably thought. Jesus has been right about many things but on this one He has missed it. The fisherman steeled himself to remain faithful to Jesus—even if it had a bitter end.

After Jesus was arrested in the garden, Peter followed the soldiers at a distance. He wanted to be near Jesus, but three times when other people said, "You were with Jesus," Peter denied it.

I can only try and imagine the pain Peter felt. He

did exactly as Jesus had predicted, and the exact opposite of what Peter had determined in his heart. As Peter denied Jesus for the third time, saying, "Man, I don't know what you are saying," the rooster crowed and Jesus looked across the courtyard at Peter. When the eyes of the two men connected, it must have filled Peter with deep sadness. His fears had been realized. Peter had failed.

But fear and failure are both terminal only when we give up. Those who press on can overcome. And both Jonah and Peter stayed around to experience God's forgiving love and grace.

After Jesus had risen from the dead, the Lord met His disciples on the beach. They had been out fishing all night, and they had breakfast with the Lord. When Jesus talked with Peter, He said, "Feed my sheep."

In the end, Peter conquered his fear. He preached the Good News on the day of Pentecost in Jerusalem and when the soldiers hauled Peter in front of the teachers of the law. The teachers were amazed at his knowledge of the Scriptures, because he had been with Jesus. Peter became one of the great leaders in the early church.

The example of Peter is an encouragement to us as well. When we honestly face some of the situations we've "run away" from, it's good to know that in only a few more steps we will meet up with God's forgiving mercy.

*Lord, today, I may feel like running away but thank You that I can press on and into Your grace and forgiveness.* ■

**REFLECT**

Someone said, "Even the whale had to suffer indigestion because of Jonah's disobedience." Who else has suffered because of your "running away," or because of your not facing your fears?

_____

_____

_____

"**A big part of being a man in today's world is facing and overcoming what I fear, even when it hurts emotionally.**"

# *Two Better Than One*

> **W**e need other men in our lives rather than believing that we can make it on our own.

**1 CORINTHIANS 10:11–13**
*Now all these things happened to them as examples, and they were written for our admonition, on whom the ends of the ages have come.*

*Therefore let him who thinks he stands take heed lest he fall.*

*No temptation has overtaken you except such as is common to man; but God is faithful, who will not allow you to be tempted beyond what you are able, but with the temptation will also make the way of escape, that you may be able to bear it.*

In *Fathers and Sons* Gordon Dalby uses a word picture that is very descriptive of where many of us are today. He says, "The wolf loves the lone sheep." Men have a tendency to "go it alone"—to handle things without help from anyone else. And the wolf, according to Dalby, is the biblical wolf—Satan himself. He thinks this is why so many men, including our leaders, are being lured "out from the fold into destruction." The image of the man as a loner has done more to destroy our manhood than anything else.

It doesn't take too much imagination to picture the scene. One of the sheep decides that he doesn't need the rest of the flock. Or perhaps the sheep feels hurt by something someone said or did, and doesn't want to confront what happened, so he just slows down his pace as he reflects alone on his situation.

Soon the flock moves farther down the path, and when the wolf comes out of the scrubs for the lone sheep, there is no place to run. The aloneness that felt so comfortable and controllable has set the sheep up for destruction.

When something doesn't go well at work, what do you do? Do you have a male friend to talk to about your difficulties with your boss, or your struggles with loving your wife, or your distant feelings towards God?

Even though we know that no one goes through life unscathed, we still feel the need to act as if we can. We feel that if we admit our woundedness to another, we will somehow be at a disadvantage. Life in the workplace is often like that—any sign of weakness and someone is willing to step on us to their own advantage. But what does God tell us to do in that situation? He wants us to be open and honest about our difficulties. And His warning is clear—if we have everyone fooled into thinking that we are standing, we are about to fall. Solomon warns against our "go it alone" attitude when he said, "Two are better than one, . . . for if they fall, one will lift up his companion. But woe to him who is alone when he falls for he has no one to help him up" (Ecc. 4:9–10).

Part of our journey towards deeper manhood means working together with a group of men. There is nothing magical about talking together—it's all spelled out in Ecclesiastes. We need men as companions on the journey to deeper manhood. No one else will do.

 **REFLECT**

Think about how you are going to handle the struggle of the days ahead. List the names of those men who will be there for you.

_____

_____

_____

 **REFLECT**

List some of the ways you have been limited or controlled by your fears.

_____

_____

_____

**"The image of the man as a loner has done more to destroy our manhood than anything else."**

*Jesus, bring a male friend into my life with whom I can share my joys and struggles. Or (if you have such a friend), Thank You, Lord for _____ and his presence in my life to share good and bad times.* ∎

# Wrestling with Woundedness

**REFLECT**

We want to look like we have it together, but underneath we have
weaknesses and areas of woundedness. Describe two of yours:

_____

_____

_____

_____

**REFLECT**

Think about the long-range impact
of this weakness on your life.

_____

_____

_____

_____

> **S**ometimes the only way we can face others is in a position of weakness, not strength. The Lord can use our weaknesses for His glory.

GENESIS 32:24–26
*Then Jacob was left alone; and a Man wrestled with him until the breaking of day.*

*Now when He saw that He did not prevail against him, He touched the socket of his hip; and the socket of Jacob's hip was out of joint as He wrestled with him.*

*And He said, "Let Me go, for the day breaks." But he said, "I will not let You go unless You bless me!"*

**A**s men, we are fragile mortals. That's not a negative statement, it is simply a fact that we would rather ignore. In his book *Fire in the Belly*, Sam Keen pointed out that "from the beginnings of recorded human history to the present day the most important tacit instruction boys receive about manhood is: Masculinity requires a wounding of the body, a sacrifice of the natural endowment of sensuality and sexuality."

Wounding the body was a requirement to become a man in biblical culture. Men had the physical wound of circumcision. In other cultures, the rite of passage from boyhood into manhood also requires some sort of physical wounding, from the loss of a tooth, to tattoos, and even to cuts that create lifetime scars.

An example of the meaning of woundedness is Jacob. On his way home, he remembered why he left in the first place—Esau was going to kill him. When he found out that Esau was coming to meet his people with 400 men, Jacob was worried and afraid. He divided his large group into two sections so that if one group was attacked, the other could escape. Jacob also tried to bribe Esau into feeling good about him by giving Esau a large gift of goats, sheep, camels, cows, and donkeys.

After all of these preparations, Jacob retired to his tent to wait for Esau, alone with his pain. He probably faced the possibility that tomorrow he would die. Did he think of suicide as the ultimate slap in his brother's face? We don't know, but for some reason God sent an angel to confront him.

Jacob and the angel wrestled throughout the night. Neither one was able to overpower the other. When dawn broke over the horizon, the angel merely touched Jacob's hip and dislocated it. But Jacob wouldn't release the angel, until he received a blessing.

I've always wondered why the angel wrestled with Jacob and ultimately dislocated his hip. Perhaps God, knowing that Jacob was such a dreamer, took physical action so that Jacob would know it was not a dream. Perhaps God also understood that the only way Jacob could meet his brother was in a position of weakness, not strength. For the rest of his life, Jacob limped as a reminder of his woundedness and his blessedness.

Others, including his brother Esau, saw the effect of Jacob's wound. But Jacob also discovered an important lesson that each of us can apply in our woundedness. Through the weakness of his leg, Jacob was reminded of his courage to go ahead and meet Esau. The Apostle Paul also learned the same principle when he told the Corinthians that God's "strength is made perfect in weakness" (2 Cor. 12:9). Through our weaknesses, we can be made strong.

*Lord, I know I have some weaknesses but I find it difficult to see how these could be turned into strengths. Give me Your insight.* ■

## REFLECT

How could God use your weaknesses to show His strength? Dream and explore the amazing surprises of God.

_____

_____

_____

"**The strength of true manhood is found in the weakness of our woundedness.**"

# *Strength Through Weakness*

## REFLECT

How have you been wounded in
your life? What are some of the
deep hurts that have left their scars?
Use a few words to describe them.

_____

_____

_____

## REFLECT

In what ways has your woundedness confronted you with your humanity, your weakness, your
limitations?

_____

_____

_____

> **O**ur weaknesses can
> keep our life in proper
> perspective. Through
> our weaknesses we can
> be strong in Christ.

ISAIAH 40:29–31
*He gives power to the weak,*
*And to those who have no might He increases strength.*
*Even the youths shall faint and be weary,*
*And the young men shall utterly fall,*
*But those who wait on the LORD*
*Shall renew their strength;*
*They shall mount up with wings like eagles,*
*They shall run and not be weary,*
*They shall walk and not faint.*

**F**rank is a real man's man. Working long
hours, Frank is in a construction trade,
working on a high-rise building in downtown Los
Angeles. He looks like a confident fellow, and when
he walks down the street, you can tell that Frank is
in excellent physical shape. Yet Sue, Frank's wife, is
fed up with the male showmanship. Initially, Sue
was attracted to the manly appearance of Frank. He
was strong and able to do many practical
skills around the house. Because of his job
he comes home covered with dirt from
head to toe, and most evenings he lies exhausted in front of the television set.
Now, after ten years of marriage, Sue
would do practically anything to get a bit
of softness and kindness from him.

When I talked with Frank about the
needs of his wife, Frank admitted that
he'd like to loosen up and be more gentle
and compassionate. He is sincere about wanting to
be different—yet at the same time, the thought of
changing scares him. Where does he begin? Will he
turn into a weakling? What will he have to give up
to make such changes in his life?

As men we struggle with the idea of paradox. How can something that contradicts itself be true? How can we be strong when we are weak? From an early age, we are taught that we can only be strong by being physically and emotionally superior. So we work very hard to conceal our weaknesses and our woundedness.

Our wounds can come from a number of sources. Our parents, other people, our culture, our economic conditions, our ethnic group, the government, even nature—all of these can inflict wounds upon us. Our wound may or may not be physical, but it will always be emotional. The wounds will always confront us with our humanness and our limitations. Our self-image will be changed.

Jacob believed in his own strength. Why, he even thought that he could wrestle with an angel and win—and he almost did! But what went through his mind when the angel simply touched his hip and it was dislocated? Is that the moment he became aware of the supernatural nature of his foe? In Hebrew, Jacob's name means *Deceiver*. Throughout his life, Jacob had always manipulated his way out of every jam, until this one. Now he was wounded for life. Whenever he put pressure on that leg, his limp reminded him of his frailty. His wound put his life into the proper perspective. Our wounds can do the same.

What strengths have you discovered because of your woundedness?

_____

_____

_____

" **God always does things His way. That is why He delights in demonstrating His strength through our weakness.** "

*Thank You for the weaknesses in my life, Lord. Use them as strengths.* ■

# Success Will Not Protect

**REFLECT**

Remember a time when you were pushed to the limit. What were the results?

_____

_____

_____

**REFLECT**

How can you work through the wounds of that experience? Perhaps you were depressed or discouraged. Can you think of some means to heal those wounds, such as friendship, counseling, or honest self-examination?

_____

_____

_____

> **W**e need to guard the successes of our life— even in success we need to acknowledge our need for the Lord.

1 KINGS 19:1–3
*And [King] Ahab told Jezebel all that Elijah had done, also how he had executed all the prophets with the sword.*

*Then Jezebel sent a messenger to Elijah, saying, "So let the gods do to me, and more also, if I do not make your life as the life of one of them by tomorrow about this time."*

*And when he saw that, he arose and ran for his life, and went to Beersheba which belongs to Judah, and left his servant there.*

The dictionary tells us that a wound is a "division of tissue or rupture . . . not caused by disease." A second definition for wound is "an injury or hurt to feelings, sensibilities, reputation."

The mighty prophet Elijah had a wound that was an injury to his reputation, although at the same time he was afraid that he would soon lose his head. It's somewhat surprising that Elijah believed in the power of Jezebel—especially when you consider the events in Elijah's life only a few hours before. It had to have been one of his high points.

Three years before, Elijah had predicted a drought in Israel. Not a drop of rain fell, and there was famine throughout the land. Elijah proposed a contest between the 450 prophets of Baal and himself.

They made two sacrifices—one to Baal and one to God. For the entire day, the prophets of Baal tried to get a response from their god, but nothing happened. Then, toward the evening, Elijah prepared a sacrifice for God. To make God's miracle appear even more impossible, he had twelve pots of water poured over the sacrifice. Then Elijah prayed a simple prayer, and fire swooped down from heaven and consumed the sacrifice, the wood, and the water. All of the people fell on their faces in fear and worship. Elijah took the reins of leadership and commanded the deaths of all the false prophets.

Elijah's faith, courage, and leadership were unmatched—that is, until later in the day, when a messenger from Jezebel threatened Elijah with his life. Elijah was a doer, an activist. Perhaps that is part of what made him so vulnerable to being wounded by Jezebel.

On the surface, it's hard to understand why he fled in terror. Only hours before he had not only defeated the false prophets of Baal, he had had them destroyed. After the execution of the prophets, Elijah announced to King Ahab that it was going to rain again in Israel— the three-year drought was over. Heavy rains fell throughout the country. So why was Elijah so terrified by Jezebel's threat?

Part of the reason could have been his exhaustion. When we push ourselves to the limit, we are vulnerable to discouragement, self-pity, and depression. Perhaps Elijah was so shocked by Jezebel's threat, he couldn't recover.

Elijah was like so many of us. We can stand up to our boss, the cop on the corner, the guy at the service station, or most any other man, but keep us away from an enraged, vengeful woman. Perhaps the prophet carried a wound from his youth that related to a woman, and Jezebel scratched off a deep scab.

Whatever the reason for Elijah's fear, one thing is clear: Success is never a protection against our being wounded or defeated. In fact, as we are successful, we need to heighten our guard. Success can set us up for a bout of self-sufficiency that ignores God's role in our lives.

*Lord, take my successes*
*and use them for Your*
*glory. Thank You for Your*
*daily presence in my life.* ■

**REFLECT**

Have you been experiencing success in your life? Describe those areas briefly.

_____

_____

_____

**REFLECT**

Success isn't a protection against wounds. Consider how can you prevent a bout of self-sufficiency in your life.

_____

_____

_____

"**God always meets us in the wounded parts of our life.**"

# Small Voices

**What are some of the ways you stay busy?**

_____

_____

_____

**What happens inside of you when you slow down? Do you sleep, watch TV, or read?**

_____

_____

_____

> **W**e need to escape the whirlwind of activity and listen to the still small voice of God.

1 KINGS 19:11–12

_Then He said, "Go out, and stand on the mountain before the LORD." And behold, the LORD passed by, and a great and strong wind tore into the mountains and broke the rocks in pieces before the LORD, but the LORD was not in the wind; and after the wind an earthquake, but the LORD was not in the earthquake; and after the earthquake a fire, but the LORD was not in the fire; and after the fire a still small voice._

**W**hen Jezebel threatened Elijah with his life, he left his servant and ran into the wilderness. He ran for a whole day and then plopped himself down under a tree. He prayed that the Lord would take his life—just end it right there under the tree. Quickly Elijah fell asleep until an angel touched him and said, "Get up and eat." After eating, Elijah sat down again and fell asleep. A second time, the angel came with food and drink for Elijah. The angel commanded, "Eat, because the journey is too great for you." Then Elijah continued running. From the strength of that food, the prophet continued for forty days and nights.

Finally, he reached Mt. Horeb and curled up in a cave and slept again. This story points out three false solutions to our woundedness—to run, to sleep, and to eat.

God didn't tell Elijah to flee anywhere, let alone run all the way to Mt. Horeb. But when Elijah ran, God didn't stay behind. During this time when Elijah was wounded, God took this opportunity to teach the prophet some important lessons about maturity and manhood. While Elijah was hiding in the cave, the Lord asked, "What are you doing here, Elijah?"

Elijah answered with a list of activities. "Look, Lord, at how much I've done for You. But every other prophet is dead. I'm the only one left." The prophet was wounded and discouraged.

God didn't answer Elijah dramatically. He was not in the winds, the earthquake, or the fire that passed by Elijah. Instead, God spoke to him in the quietness of a whisper: words of strength and encouragement. Elijah's perception of the situation was wrong. He wasn't the only prophet left in Israel. But God's whisper was probably the last place Elijah expected to hear God. After all, Elijah was a man used to the spectacular and the dramatic, like the sacrifice on Mount Carmel.

One of my friends, Bill, felt as if his life was on a treadmill of activity. Bill's daily schedule was filled with appointments, meetings, important deadlines, and family obligations. Like a master juggler, Bill was constantly throwing balls into the air. But the hectic pace of Bill's life quickened, and someone kept throwing more balls into his act. Because of his leadership skills, Bill was elected to the board of the church, which meant more meetings and more responsibility. Since he was active in his son's school program, Bill served on a couple of committees at school.

One day, the whirlwind of activity came to a screeching halt. Bill felt some pains along his arm and interrupted an appointment to see a doctor. "You've had a mild heart attack. You're twenty-five pounds overweight and need to change your lifestyle," the doctor told him. Pain caught Bill's attention and he began to stop the busyness. For Bill, the pain in his arm was like a still, small voice.

In our running and in our busyness, the still, small voice often goes unheard. Yet we must stop to hear it.

*Lord, life seems like a merry-go-round. Help me get off and listen to your still small voice.* ∎

**REFLECT**

In what ways might your busyness keep you from hearing God's still small voice?

_____

_____

_____

**REFLECT**

Describe two or three things you could begin doing in order to slow down the pace of your life.

_____

_____

_____

"**God will meet us wherever we are.**"

# *Sense of Powerlessness*

**REFLECT**

How have you attempted to rationalize some of your woundedness?

_____

_____

_____

**REFLECT**

As you consider these areas of woundedness, have you reacted through anger and hostility? How?

_____

_____

_____

**W**e need to learn from our wounds and not strike out in anger because of our sense of powerlessness.

JOB 29:10–12
*The voice of the nobles was hushed,*
*And their tongue stuck to the roof of their mouth.*
*When the ear heard, then it blessed me,*
*And when the eye saw, then it approved me;*
*Because I delivered the poor who cried out,*
*And the fatherless and he who had no helper.*

**T**he Bible doesn't tell us anything about Job's father. We don't know whether he was a good man who spent a lot of time with his son, or whether he was absent, either emotionally or literally. Let's assume that Job had a good relationship with his father. The result was that Job was a man who was comfortable with his manhood.

As we have learned, it's not only our fathers who can wound us; a number of other people and events can hurt us as well. Job is an example of a man who is deeply wounded, not by issues with his father, but by the circumstances of his life. Life dealt him a terrible blow, much like life does to some of us. A car accident, the loss of a job, a wife that walks out of our life—any of these events can make us one of the wounded.

William is one of my friends who for many years has been in the construction business in Orange County, California. When the economic recession hit, the construction business dried up and my friend struggled to survive financially. Ultimately he lost his business and had to file for bankruptcy. In the middle of his financial woes, his wife ran off with another man. She found someone who would listen with fresh ears to her concerns and cares. Like a magnet, the new person drew her away from her long-term marriage to my friend.

A lost business and a lost marriage. Each one for

this man came through circumstances outside of his control. How do you respond when it happens to you or to a friend of yours?

The typical male response is, "Life goes on—after all, it was only a job," or "I'm better off without her," or "I can always get another car." We have been taught to ignore the wound and act as if it doesn't exist, as if the pain doesn't really hurt that bad. If we do permit ourselves to feel sadness for what has been lost, we usually become nostalgic for the "good old days." That's what Job was doing in the chapter for today's Bible reading. He cried out, "Oh, that I were as in months past."

We usually try to ignore our woundedness by either holding on to the past, or by working at creating a new future. We want to be anywhere but in the present. The here and now is where we hurt. At times like these, God seems far away from us. If we don't allow ourselves to experience the pain in the present, we see ourselves cut off—from ourselves, from those who care about us, and from God.

Another part of our process in facing our woundedness is the awareness of intense anger within, and the desire to lash out even at those who are being sympathetic to us. That's part of the myth we have been taught about manliness—we are to get angry when we are hurt. In *The Masculine Journey* Robert Hicks points out that when we have been "wounded by society or circumstances, by parent or spouse, the hostile male feels powerless and so strikes out. The hostile spirit is rooted in woundedness."

The root of most of our anger is the sense of powerlessness. We have never really learned the lesson that manliness is found within our powerlessness. Job's wounds were so deep and so pervasive, he had no choice but to learn.

*Lord, I don't want to hurt others through my anger over my sense of powerlessness. Help me to channel that negative energy into my own growth.* ∎

**REFLECT**

How can you use this sense of powerlessness to your advantage? Can you think of ways to convert the anger into a positive dependence on the Lord?

_____

_____

_____

"**Out of our woundedness can come healing and strength.**"

# Unexamined Wounds

**REFLECT**

Describe some of the wounds you received from your father and his father.

_____

_____

_____

**REFLECT**

Describe some of the wounds you have received from life—from the job, accidents, wife, friend, relatives, coaches, teachers, peers.

_____

_____

_____

**W**ounds can hurt but unless they are faced and healed, we will pass them on to future generations.

JOB 19:1–4

*Then Job answered and said: "How long will you*
*    torment my soul,*
*And break me in pieces with words?*
*These ten times you have reproached me;*
*You are not ashamed that you have wronged me.*
*And if indeed I have erred,*
*My error remains with me.*

**W**ho taught you how to hold a bat, boy? Did you figure that out all by yourself? This is a team sport!" the baseball coach screamed into the face of the shriveling six-year-old. This kid had a lot to learn and he knew it. Unfortunately, the coach was full of his own problems and had no idea how to encourage players. He majored in discouragement and destruction of self-worth. For the boy, the wounds went deep. He wondered if he would ever play a sport with some degree of success. For many years, this boy bore emotional scars.

"Some assignment," the high school student muttered. "If the teacher wanted to rewrite my paper, why did I do it in the first place?" As he turned toward his locker, the boy crumpled several sheets of paper. The writing assignment was covered with red marks from the teacher. Although it was a single day of homework, this boy took it as something more. He wondered if he could ever write a decent paper—one that was praised and not destroyed. With one sweep, this boy's self-confidence was wounded.

"Does your mom help you with this?" a father glanced down at his watch. His second-grader was only starting to read on his own and it was painfully slow and difficult. Like listening to a recording on a slow speed, the father wanted to crank up the pace. Over and over, the father helped his son with the next word. The father had no patience to listen to his child sounding out the words and making sense on his own. Finally, in frustration, the boy threw the book on the floor. "I'll never learn to read," he shouted as he left the room. That evening of homework would haunt the son for years—could he ever make sense of the letters on the page and learn to read?

In today's Bible reading, Job felt the deep wounds to his body. Job had physical sores, his children had been killed, and his wealth had been destroyed. Job didn't understand the wounds that had been heaped on his life. Throughout the book of Job, he reflects and asks, "Why?"

"Why?" is a fair question, but sometimes it doesn't have any clear-cut answers. As we noted yesterday, sometimes our wounds come about simply through the unfairness of life. Maybe a coach didn't take a few extra minutes. Or a teacher was exhausted and having a bad day, so he decided to pass his pain on to his students through destructive comments and red marks on homework. Or a tired father didn't want to read with his son but was forced into the role because his wife had a meeting at church. Somebody had to help the boy with his homework. But that somebody, that dad, didn't give the assignment the energy and attention it deserved. Instead, the comments left wounds on the boy.

When these wounds are left untreated, they become part of the baggage we transfer to the next generation, and to those beyond, until someone stops the pattern. Thankfully, you can stop that cycle of destruction and make a difference.

*Lord, I want to break the cycle of woundedness. Help me to take some action today to treat my wounds.* ■

**REFLECT**

**What are some of the ways you have ignored your wounds, leaving then to fester and grow?**

_____

_____

_____

**REFLECT**

**In what wounds have you experienced some healing?**

_____

_____

_____

**"To feel safe in surviving our wounds, we need the friendship of other men who are also dealing with their wounds."**

# Coming to Terms

**REFLECT**

**Who has inflicted the greatest wounds upon you? What are the more recent ones? The deepest ones?**

_____

_____

_____

**REFLECT**

**Describe how it feels to admit that you are weak or powerless.**

_____

_____

_____

JOB 42:3–6
_"You asked, 'Who is this who hides counsel without
   knowledge?'_
_Therefore I have uttered what I did not understand,_
_Things too wonderful for me, which I did not know._
_Listen, please, and let me speak;_
_You said, 'I will question you, and you shall answer
   Me.'_
_"I have heard of You by the hearing of the ear,_
_But now my eye sees You._
_Therefore I abhor myself, and repent in dust and ashes."_

**E**ach of us is human and has a frail and weak side. Often we don't expose that self to others or even to ourselves. It takes great courage to reveal this side of ourselves.

Once I listened a speech from Dr. C. Everett Koop, then the Surgeon General of the United States. Dr. Koop told about losing his son when he died in a mountain climbing accident. "I saw afresh that God is sovereign, and looked ahead and saw His majesty and power."

As I sat in the audience, something made me balk. _How can you say that about God when you lost your son—something that is so precious to you?_ But Dr. Koop had learned from the biblical model of Job. He had learned to look beyond the immediate pain of the situation and through it to the broader plan of God for his life and his son's life.

Typically, manliness has been defined as strength. But the biblical concept of manliness means that we be aware and incorporate our own weaknesses. If your masculinity has no room for weakness or powerlessness, then you've got a pseudo-masculinity which only creates additional problems both inside and with your relationships.

We may never understand why the wound occurred—Job never did. But we must learn whatever

> **E**ach of us, like Job, must come to terms with our limitations as men.

is important for us to gain from our wound. For Job it meant a whole new understanding of the nature and purpose of God in Job's life.

I have always been struck by the fact that God never tells Job why he suffered. And what is even more amazing is that by the end of the book, Job has dropped his concerns about why he suffered. Something far more important happened to him.

When God finally responded to Job, he gave no answers. The Lord only asked questions and his questions for the most part were still unanswerable. All through the later stages of the story, God asked Job questions, and then pressed him for answers, much like Job had done with God. Job's only response was to tell God that "I lay my hand over my mouth" (Job 40:4). But God continued his questions. When He finally stopped, Job said, "I abhor myself, and repent in dust and ashes" (Job 42:6).

Throughout the book, Job questioned God. But he never overstepped the boundary between himself and God. Then why did Job repent? It seems clear that, for the first time, Job saw God as He really was—all-powerful.

At the same time, Job saw himself as he really was—weak and wounded. He repented of his failure to see his frailty and God's majesty. Later, in the last chapter of Job, God again affirmed the fact that Job said nothing wrong (see 42:7). So the distortion of perception was the only thing for which Job could repent.

Somehow each of us, like Job, must come to terms with our limitations as men. In the military, when a man is wounded he is given a purple heart. Veterans who have been awarded a purple heart wear it with pride, and those who see it on their chests and understand its meaning treat them with honor and respect. Instead of hiding our wounds, we need to learn how to talk about our wounds with other wounded men.

> *I'd like to have the courage to face my own frailties and limitations. Give me that strength for today.* ■

**REFLECT**

Describe the ways you have either ignored your wounds, minimized them, or made them worse.

_____

_____

_____

**REFLECT**

Describe what you are doing to slow your pace of life so that you can find healing for your woundedness.

_____

_____

_____

**"We may never understand why the wound occurred—Job never did."**

# *The Path of Grief*

**When was the last time you grieved? Describe the situation.**

_____

_____

_____

**When was a recent time when others were falling apart and crying, but you felt it was your manly duty to remain strong? What did you do with those feelings?**

_____

_____

_____

> **In our journey to true manhood, we need to reflect on our losses and learn to grieve.**

MATTHEW 5:3–10
*Blessed are the poor in spirit,*
*For theirs is the kingdom of heaven.*
*Blessed are those who mourn,*
*For they shall be comforted.*
*Blessed are the meek,*
*For they shall inherit the earth.*
*Blessed are those who hunger and thirst for*
*righteousness,*
*For they shall be filled.*
*Blessed are the merciful,*
*For they shall obtain mercy.*
*Blessed are the pure in heart,*
*For they shall see God.*
*Blessed are the peacemakers,*
*For they shall be called the sons of God.*
*Blessed are those who are persecuted for*
*righteousness' sake,*
*For theirs is the kingdom of heaven.*

When we are wounded in any way, we feel pain. When we feel pain, we need to express to someone what we are experiencing. That goes counter to what many of us have been taught about manhood. Usually men have two feelings—either "I feel good" or "I feel bad." But true manhood knows how to grieve.

In *Iron John*, Robert Bly comments on the fact that, generally speaking, men don't know how to grieve. When men think of grief, we think of funerals—that's when we grieve. But the emotion of grief is associated with *any* kind of loss. It can be a person, but it can also be anything else that matters to us.

One of my friends, Mark, weeps every time he talks about his father, who died when Mark was nine years old. His mother and sister fell apart, so Mark acted like a "man"; he was strong and hid whatever emotions he was feeling at the time. Now, as an adult, the only time Mark experiences sadness is when he talks about his father. The rest of the time Mark feels and acts angry.

Mark remembered the sense of powerlessness that he felt when his dad died. What he couldn't see was the connection between his continuing sense of powerlessness in most areas of his life and the anger he always seemed to be carrying.

We often think that because we know how to experience anger, we are connected to our feelings. But the anger most of us feel is a replacement for the grief and sadness that blocks us from not only our emotions but also from our manhood.

When we read through the Beatitudes, we don't find much that correlates with the modern definition of masculinity. Jesus is talking about mourning, meekness, and peacemaking. What does that have to do with being a man in today's world?

Rather than attempt to remold our concept of manhood, we simply reject what Jesus is saying and believe those sections of the Bible are for someone else. But the Beatitudes are a part of true masculinity. We are blessed when we are poor in spirit. We are blessed when we know how to mourn. Grieving leads us into a true poverty of spirit and brings us to a place where God meets us and blesses us.

If we are going to awaken from our emotional numbness, the doorway to that awakening is through grief, not through anger. We may encounter anger in the process, but most of our anger will only serve to keep people at a distance. Healing within begins as we begin to grieve.

*Lord, give me the strength as a man to feel grief and learn to handle feelings of sadness. Help this be one of my steps toward healing.* ■

**REFLECT**

What steps can you take to give yourself permission to grieve and mourn? It's okay to feel sadness.

_____

_____

_____

**"If we are going to awaken from our emotional numbness, the doorway to that awakening is through grief, not through anger."**

# *Identify Your Losses*

**What are some of your losses? Identify those you have experienced in relation to your father.**

_____

_____

_____

**What are some other important losses you have experienced?**

_____

_____

_____

> **B**ecoming more aware of our emotions will almost always begin with the feeling of sadness.

MARK 14:32–36

*Then they came to a place which was named Gethsemane; and He said to His disciples, "Sit here while I pray."*

*And He took Peter, James, and John with Him, and He began to be troubled and deeply distressed. Then He said to them, "My soul is exceedingly sorrowful, even to death. Stay here and watch."*

*He went a little farther, and fell on the ground, and prayed that if it were possible, the hour might pass from Him. And He said, "Abba, Father, all things are possible for You. Take this cup away from Me; nevertheless, not what I will, but what You will."*

**S**ometimes it is hard to identify what we have lost and so we don't know how or where to begin to grieve. A good starting place is to look at some of our unfulfilled expectations. What didn't we receive as a boy and what have we created to fill the place of those missing things?

The father of my friend Mark died when he was nine years old. Since Mark didn't understand how to grieve his loss, his feelings of sadness erupted in anger.

Now as a man, Mark has his own children. He understands from personal experience that he missed a lot of time with his dad. To compensate for his loss, Mark fills his spare time with his children. He spends time playing indoor games with them during the winter months or curled up with them to read a good story aloud. Then, in the summer, the outdoor activities are in full swing and Mark takes an active role in their sports. He makes time to practice with them in his backyard. But deep inside, Mark knows he is missing something. *It will be different for my kids,* he keeps telling himself.

Mark is attempting to fill a void his father left with the activities of his children. Once Mark was able to understand this dynamic in his life, it gave him a place to begin to identify his losses and deal with them in balance.

As Christians, we have a supernatural Father to turn to with our grief and losses. In the final hours of the life of Jesus, He turned to His heavenly Father in prayer at the Garden of Gethsemane. Jesus was in deep distress and sadness. He wanted to escape the sorrow. God could remove His sorrow so He didn't have to go through the experience of dying on a cross. But instead, Jesus prayed, "Nevertheless, not what I will, but what You will." Jesus could deal with His loss and the experiences in the days ahead through the grace and mercy of God, the Father.

The importance of Mark's time with his children was an indicator to him of what he had lost when his father died. He looked further at what types of things were of primary importance for him to share with his children. From this he had a place to begin to identify what he had lost.

As we understand and feel our grief or losses, it is the first step toward replacing them in our lives. Like Jesus, we can begin to deal with the grief that we face by turning to the heavenly Father. God knows our struggles inside out and listens at a moment's notice.

*I know I've experienced losses in my life, Lord. Give me Your insight as to how I've faced them and replaced them.* ■

**REFLECT**

**What have you done to grieve these losses?**

_____

_____

_____

**REFLECT**

**Allow yourself some time to think about and *feel* your past losses. Which ones are unfinished?**

_____

_____

_____

> **"We need to understand and feel our grief and losses so we will understand how we have replaced them in our lives."**

# *A* Doorway to Understanding

How do you express the range of emotions in your life? Think about a sad situation and describe it below.

_____

_____

_____

Think about a time when you have had great joy in your life. Describe it below.

_____

_____

_____

**K**nowing ourselves involves knowing our emotions.

2 SAMUEL 19:5–8
*Then Joab came into the house to the king, and said, "Today you have disgraced all your servants who today have saved your life, the lives of your sons and daughters, the lives of your wives and the lives of your concubines, in that you love your enemies and hate your friends. For you have declared today that you regard neither princes nor servants; for today I perceive that if Absalom had lived and all of us had died today, then it would have pleased you well."*

*"Now therefore, arise, go out and speak comfort to your servants. For I swear by the LORD, if you do not go out, not one will stay with you this night. And that will be worse for you than all the evil that has befallen you from your youth until now."*

*Then the king arose and sat in the gate. And they told all the people, saying, "There is the king, sitting in the gate." So all the people came before the king. For everyone of Israel had fled to his tent.*

**K**ing David was a man who knew how to get in touch with his emotions. Those emotions fill the pages of Scripture, especially in the book of Psalms. He also knew how to grieve, even at the expense of his reputation.

David loved Absalom, but Absalom took revenge on Amnon and fled for his life. When Absalom wanted to return home, one of the conditions that David set was that Absalom could not see or speak to his father (2 Sam. 14:24). Yet when Absalom was invited back to Jerusalem and Absalom attempted a coup against his father, David was only concerned for Absalom's safety—even at the expense of his own kingdom (2 Sam. 18:4). And when he learned that Absalom died in the conflict, David grieved.

We may be critical of David for his aloofness towards his children, and consider him a failure as a father for the way he treated Absalom by isolating him and refusing to talk things through. But David knew how to grieve. He was never embarrassed by the expression of emotion.

When David heard of his son's death, he wept and mourned, even to the point that Joab had to remind him that he was confusing the people. Although Absalom was a son, he was also the king's enemy in battle.

At another time, when the Ark of the Covenant was being brought back into Jerusalem, David led the procession, and in his emotional exuberance, he danced in a way that embarrassed his wife Michal (see 2 Sam. 6:12–23). All through the Psalms, David expressed a wide range of emotions, from great joy to deep depression, guilt, and fear. He was comfortable with his manhood, and he was comfortable with his emotions. There is a connection between the two concepts.

Only when we can know what we feel, and are able to describe and express it, can we come to know our deeper masculine nature. And the doorway to understanding our emotional makeup is to become comfortable with grieving. Our grief can come in many forms—not just at the death of someone we love, but also when we lose something that we treasure.

**REFLECT**

When was the last time that you were depressed or sad? Describe it below.

_____

_____

_____

**REFLECT**

When was the last time that a situation stirred you with excitement and anticipation? Describe the details below.

_____

_____

_____

> "David was never embarrassed by the expression of emotion."

*Lord, I know I have the full range of emotions but help me to express them.* ∎

# *Separating Men from Boys*

**REFLECT**

In what ways have some of your losses made you feel that you have also lost status?

_____

_____

_____

**REFLECT**

Describe some events in your life that have been very humbling.

_____

_____

_____

> **I learn more about trusting when I trust myself to look at the darker experiences of my life.**

PSALM 40:1–3
*I waited patiently for the LORD;
And He inclined to me,
And heard my cry.
He also brought me up out of a horrible pit,
Out of the miry clay,
And set my feet upon a rock,
And established my steps.
He has put a new song in my mouth—
Praise to our God;
Many will see it and fear,
And will trust in the LORD.*

The phone rings in the middle of the night. From a dead sleep, you reach out and pick it up with a bit of trembling. What could have happened to merit such a call? In a split second, your mind races through the possibilities—a sudden death of a parent, a crisis from an adult child, or an accident involving someone close to you. Then you hear the dreaded words, "I'm sorry to be the one to tell you but . . ." Suddenly you are jarred from your bed to action. Feelings of grief overwhelm you, but you only stay with the feeling for a minute. "Okay, I'm tough. I can handle it . . ." You stuff the feeling of loss and grief deep inside and begin to make a practical plan for the next steps. While planning and motion is necessary, it is also important to feel the grief and sadness.

The path of sorrow and grieving separates the men from the boys. Yet as I've watched some of my friends "become men" through grief, I have been frightened by the process. A big part of me doesn't want to do it. Even if I am confronted with grief over some loss, I don't want to look at it very long. "I'll just cut my losses and move on down the road" is the approach that I sometimes take.

If we stuff those feelings into a bag that we throw into a corner of our hearts, we don't examine them very long. We're afraid if we dwell on the feelings, we will lose our sense of "specialness." One moment from the outside we appear to have it together, then in a moment it looks as if the foundation of our lives is crumbling. That can't happen to *me!* By loss, I don't necessarily mean that you have lost everything. But when we lose our specialness, it will mean some kind of loss in our status. On the inside, we are keenly aware of the loss.

Jesus knew what it was to experience loss and grief. The prophet Isaiah calls him a Man of Sorrows, acquainted with grief (See Isa. 53:3). In today's Bible reading from the Psalms, we rediscover that David is also a man who knew sorrow. Yet David knew how to articulate his feelings. David also had an intimate relationship with the living God. The Lord's thoughts toward us, according to David, are more than can be numbered. Also, God knows about our tears of sadness. In fact, according to Psalm 56:8, God saves all of our tears in a bottle. The Heavenly Father knows our situation, our loss and our grief. The wide shoulders of the Living Lord are there for us to turn to, just as they were for David.

*Lord, give me your strength and help to grow as I learn to handle my grief and loss.* ■

**REFLECT**

In either the loss of status, or the humbling of your spirit, describe how you viewed yourself before, during, and after the loss or humbling event.

_____

_____

_____

**REFLECT**

Describe the way these events still affect you.

_____

_____

_____

> **"One moment we appear to have it all together, the next moment it looks like the foundation of our lives is crumbling."**

# The Way Out Is Through

**REFLECT**

When was the last time you were depressed? Describe some of the circumstances.

_____

_____

_____

**REFLECT**

How can you break out of your depression and move toward wholeness? List a concrete step that you will take.

_____

_____

_____

PSALM 42:5–8
*Why are you cast down, O my soul?*
*And why are you disquieted within me?*
*Hope in God, for I will yet praise Him*
*For the help of His countenance.*
*O my God, my soul is cast down within me;*
*Therefore I will remember You from the land of the*
 *Jordan,*
*And from the heights of Hermon,*
*From the Hill Mizar.*
*Deep calls unto deep at the noise of Your waterfalls;*
*All Your waves and billows have gone over me.*
*The LORD will command His lovingkindness in the*
 *daytime,*
*And in the night His song shall be with me—*
*A prayer to the God of my life.*

> **T**he way out of our limitations is to grow through the grieving.

**S**aul did not know how to grieve. In the event that marked the end of his effectiveness as king, Saul begged Samuel to come and make a sacrifice with him in order to "save face" (1 Sam. 15:30). Samuel refused to go with Saul and he never saw Saul again. "Nevertheless Samuel mourned for Saul." But there is no hint that Saul mourned for the loss of God's anointing on him as king. Saul was too proud. He could never acknowledge what David so clearly described, "My soul is cast down within me."

What happened with Saul (and didn't occur within David) was a deep, long-term depression. In this depression, Saul became obsessed with killing David, believing that he is the threat to Saul's kingship. This obsession kept Saul from his family and from the balance he once had in his "kingly" work.

When we fail to grieve, the alternative is going to be depression. As men, we tend to think of depression as a deep melancholy that paralyzes us from our work. It can be experienced that way, but the way we most often experience depression is through an emotional numbness that cuts us off from real emotions.

Saul didn't know himself anymore. All he knew was that David was going to be the next king. He reasoned that if he could somehow kill David, his reign as king would be protected. Also, Saul believed that if he succeeded, then at his death his son would become king. Saul's only concern was to look good, and that didn't allow for grieving.

Saul lost touch with God after that as well. That's another consequence of our failure to grieve. We lose our connection with God. Oh, we may still go through all the motions of prayer and Bible reading, even serving others through ministry, but down inside is a coldness we don't want to acknowledge. We ignore this spiritual numbness because we don't really know what to do to change it.

Many times we have heard that "the way out is through." The way out of our numbness, both spiritually and personally, is to go through the grieving process. As we begin to grieve, we may think we are allowing ourselves to be depressed. But the difference between grieving and depression is that in grieving there is movement— we are moving forward. In depression there is sameness—day after day it is always the same empty hollow feeling. The choice is ours: grief or depression.

*Lord, I don't want to be depressed. Please teach me how to handle my emotions and learn how to grieve.* ■

**REFLECT**

Sometimes we want to move backwards and return to the past. As you look at your work or your family, how will you face the future and keep moving ahead?

_____

_____

**REFLECT**

Are you spiritually numb? What steps can you take to move away from the numbness?

_____

_____

_____

> **"The difference between grieving and depression is that in grieving there is movement— we are moving forward."**

# *Obedient Grieving*

**REFLECT**

If your wife ran away with another lover, imagine how you would handle the situation. Would it be like Hosea?

_____

_____

_____

**REFLECT**

Hosea's love for his wife is a picture of how God has loved us. What new insights does this give you about your love relationship with God the Father?

_____

_____

_____

> **W**e learn more about love when we walk the path of grief.

HOSEA 3

*Then the LORD said to me, "Go again, love a woman who is loved by a lover and is committing adultery, just like the love of the LORD for the children of Israel, who look to other gods and love the raisin cakes of the pagans."*

*So I bought her for myself for fifteen shekels of silver, and one and one-half homers of barley. And I said to her, "You shall stay with me many days; you shall not play the harlot, nor shall you have a man; thus I will also be toward you."*

*For the children of Israel shall abide many days without king or prince, without sacrifice or sacred pillar, without ephod or teraphim. Afterward the children of Israel shall return, seek the LORD their God and David their king, and fear the LORD and His goodness in the latter days.*

I've known many men whose wives have been unfaithful. When this happens, almost every man immediately ends the marriage, even those who have been unfaithful themselves. Women are much more forgiving. It's directly related to our inability to grieve as men.

A quick reading of this short chapter gives the impression that Hosea calmly did what God told him to do. His wife ran away with another man but Hosea bought her again in the market and brought her into his home.

But maybe it wasn't all calm. Use your manly imagination for a moment and think of what Hosea went through as he tried to find his wife turned prostitute. She didn't just have an affair, she made a living at it.

When Hosea found her he had to buy her, though according to scholars he paid a "bargain basement price." Any price would be too much under those circumstances, but Hosea knew something about obedience to God.

One of the ways that verse three can be understood is "You must live alone for a time, not being with other men or being a prostitute. I will wait and then we will be together." Hosea needed time to grieve what he had lost, for what he had found was vastly different from what he had dreamed of for his family.

How can we know that about Hosea? For one thing, Hosea's relationship with Gomer is presented as a metaphor for God's relationship with Israel. And God withdrew from his people in order to grieve over what they had done. It is seen woven through the message Hosea presents in the rest of his book. He speaks of judgment for their unrepentant spirit, but always in the context of love.

In *Peculiar Treasurers* Frederick Buechner notes that when Hosea stood on the street corner belting out: "How can I give you up, O Ephraim! How can I hand you over, O Israel! . . . For I am God and not man, The holy One in your midst" (Hosea 11:8–9), nobody can say how many converts Hosea made, but one thing that's for sure: There was seldom a dry eye in the house, including Gomer's. Buechner might have added, "including Hosea's." Yes, Hosea was presenting a message of judgment, but woven into it was a message of God's unfailing love.

God knows how to grieve, for we see that clearly in the life of Jesus Christ. Hosea must have known how to grieve as well. To be men, we also need to learn how to grieve.

*Lord, as I walk the path of grief, teach me to deepen my love for my family and You.* ■

Think about the persistence and means that Hosea used to locate and purchase his wife again. How has God the Father persistently pursued you?

_____

_____

_____

What can we learn about God's grief through the life of Jesus?

_____

_____

_____

"**Hosea knew something about obedience to God.**"

# Long Road of Grief

**REFLECT**

What are some of the messages you've been given about grieving, especially in relation to our need to shorten the process as men?

_____

_____

_____

**REFLECT**

Who gave you those messages about grieving?

_____

_____

_____

> **B**eing a man in today's world requires being a man comfortable with sorrow.

ROMANS 9:1–5
*I tell you the truth in Christ, I am not lying, my conscience also bearing me witness in the Holy Spirit, that I have great sorrow and continual grief in my heart.*

*For I could wish that I myself were accursed from Christ for my brethren, my kinsmen according to the flesh, who are Israelites, to whom pertain the adoption, the glory, the covenants, the giving of the law, the service of God, and the promises; of whom are the fathers and from whom, according to the flesh, Christ came, who is over all, the eternally blessed God. Amen.*

**P**aul speaks here of a great sorrow and grieving continually. The sorrow he speaks of was over the rejection of Christ by his brethren, the Israelites. Some believed that this sorrow was intensified by the rejection he had experienced from his own family, possibly even including his wife. As a Pharisee he had to have a wife. What happened to her? She could have died. But more likely, at his conversion to Christianity, his whole family would have considered Paul dead, completely cutting him off.

We don't really know, but what we do know is that Paul knew grief.

D. H. Lawrence once wrote:

I am not a mechanism, an assembly of various sections.
And it is not because the mechanism is working wrongly, that I am ill.
I am ill because of wounds to the soul, to the deep emotional self—
and the wounds to the soul take a long, long time, only time can help
and patience, and a certain difficult repentance
long difficult repentance, realization of life's mistakes, and the freeing oneself
from the endless repetition of the mistake
which mankind at large has chosen to sanctify.

When Lawrence spoke of a "long, long time," he was talking about the time for grieving. It is never short, especially when it involves wounds to our soul. One of the mistakes of the common understanding of manhood is that grieving is quick. The truth is that grieving takes whatever time it needs to take, and just as with deep wounds to our flesh, the deeper the wound the more time it takes to heal.

One of my friends had a small son who died several years ago. Time and tears have healed much in the life of this father. But even seven years later, recently this father found tears rolling down his cheeks as he thought again about his son during his final days of life. Grieving has no time frame or formula.

Paul didn't "just get over it"; he wrote of "continual grief." He became more of a man through that long grief. He also became more of God's man through that long process. We can do the same.

 **REFLECT**

Describe some of your fears of what might happen if you really allowed yourself to grieve.

_____

_____

_____

 **REFLECT**

Consider taking a risk this week. Talk about your own grief with another man.

_____

_____

_____

" **Grieving has no time frame nor formula.** "

*Give me the strength and courage to be comfortable with sorrow, Lord.* ∎

# *A Long Obedience*

**REFLECT**

Describe a time when your integrity has been compromised.

_____

_____

_____

**REFLECT**

How did you cover up for your mistake of integrity? What happened if you were caught?

_____

_____

_____

> **I**ntegrity has room for failure as long as there is an openness to the truth.

1 JOHN 2:3–6

*Now by this we know that we know Him, if we keep His commandments.*

*He who says, "I know Him," and does not keep His commandments, is a liar, and the truth is not in him.*

*But whoever keeps His word, truly the love of God is perfected in him. By this we know that we are in Him.*

*He who says he abides in Him ought himself also to walk just as He walked.*

**S**ome years ago, Eugene Peterson wrote a book entitled *A Long Obedience in the Same Direction,* based on the Psalms of Ascent. I read the book during a particularly difficult time of my life, and it had a powerful impact on me. I was questioning a lot of the basics in my life. My doctorate had just been finished. I had been an associate pastor and was beginning my work as a therapist. Peterson's book encouraged me to have a consistent walk with God.

Although some of those days were dark and I couldn't see where I was going to end up, I knew I needed to continue walking with obedience. I had struggles within my family. There was unrest in my work, and everything about life seemed unsettled. It would have been easy for me to make a bad decision and come down in the wrong place. Instead, reading this book and the Psalms got me back on track. I love Peterson's title, *A Long Obedience in the Same Direction.* By itself, it says a lot.

I believe that the Apostle John would have liked that title as well. He writes a lot about obedience, and he doesn't mince words. In 1 John 2:4 he simply says, "He who says, 'I know Him,' and doesn't keep His commandments, is a liar, and the truth is not in him." That's a black-and-white statement in a culture that wants everything to be gray.

Obedience has a lot to do with integrity, and integrity is an essential part of true manhood. The more common definition of integrity is an "uncompromising adherence to moral and ethical principles; soundness of moral character; honesty." The second definition is important as well: "the state of being whole or entire." They are really quite similar. Whenever we lose the soundness of our moral character through dishonesty, we lose our wholeness. We become less of a person in some critical way.

Unfortunately, most of us have learned about the pitfalls of compromise through personal experience. When we do something that compromises our integrity, we feel less than whole; we have lost something of ourselves.

David wrote, "Vindicate me, O LORD / For I will walk in my integrity. / I have trusted in the LORD; / I shall not slip " (Ps. 26:1). The life of King David was certainly not faultless, yet he could still talk about his integrity. How? I believe one of the keys comes in the phrase "I have trusted in the Lord." David demonstrated this trust in the Lord through his openness before the Lord. He asks God to "Examine me . . . and prove me; Try my mind and my heart" (v. 2). None of David's actions were hidden from the heart of God, and David did nothing to deny them as well. That's an important part of integrity—to know yourself and to be known by God and others.

It appears that there is more to obedience than just following the rules. In David's case, it also meant a willingness to be corrected, and an openness to admit failure and grieve over the losses. David's example of stumbling and yet readjusting and going on with a heart of integrity is an illustration that we can follow in our day to day lives.

*Help me to draw strength from You, Lord, as I seek to follow Your way every day.* ■

**REFLECT**

**To do the right action in a world that whispers *cheat, cheat,* is tough. Consider ways that you have trusted in the Lord.**

_____

_____

_____

**REFLECT**

**Integrity issues are always lurking around the next corner. Consider what lies ahead for you and plan some steps for handling the temptation with God's strength.**

_____

_____

_____

> **"When we lose the soundness of our moral character through dishonesty, we lose our wholeness."**

# Commanded to Love

**REFLECT**

What difficult decisions have you made in obedience to God, or to maintain integrity within yourself?

_____

_____

_____

**REFLECT**

What are you struggling with today that is a question of being obedient to something you know is right?

_____

_____

_____

**G**od wouldn't command us to love, if there weren't something important for us to learn in the process.

HOSEA 14:4–9
*"I will heal their backsliding,*
*I will love them freely,*
*For My anger has turned away from him. . . .*
*Ephraim shall say,*
*'What have I to do anymore with idols?'*
*I have heard and observed him.*
*I am like a green cypress tree;*
*Your fruit is found in Me."*
*Who is wise?*
*Let him understand these things.*
*Who is prudent?*
*Let him know them.*
*For the ways of the LORD are right;*
*The righteous walk in them,*
*But transgressors stumble in them.*

**M**att was one of the newest managers in his office and trying to impress his boss by showing that he was fitting in. At 5:30 he glanced at his watch. Almost everyone except the cleaning people had long disappeared. As he tossed another piece of paper into a file tray, Matt remembered that he had promised his nine-year-old son, Bobby, that he would go to his afternoon softball game. The team took to the field for practice about 5 P.M., and he knew that the game had begun right as he looked at his watch.

*Well, softball is pretty slow action,* Matt thought to himself. *I'll work a bit longer and make it to the last half of the game.* He knew it was a little compromise. But his son made a double play in the first inning and Matt would only hear about it. The incident was one more brick in the wall between father and son.

Last week, we looked at the obedience in Hosea's life. God had commanded that he marry Gomer, a prostitute. Then, when his wife ran away, Hosea obeyed God, sought out his wife, and reconciled to her. The love that Hosea showed in doing this was a love born out of commitment both to God and to her, and a decision to both obey and continue to love.

Have you ever wondered how God could make loving others a commandment? After all, how can you demand love? The conventional wisdom of the world and love songs say that love is fickle—here today and gone tomorrow. The messages from society tell us to ride the roller coaster of love up and down. And those messages bear fruit, if you believe that love is only an emotion. But there is a different point of view. Loving and loving behavior are willful choices that we can make with our daily decisions. When we understand this concept, then we can see why loving others becomes the "second great commandment."

Hosea had one of the most challenging decisions of life in his obedience to God. There was no way he could save face among his friends and neighbors and also do what God asked him to do. That decision to love became one of Hosea's wounds and also became a part of the man he was.

When John wrote about obedience, he coupled it with Jesus' command to love others. Who are you having difficulty loving? Why is it difficult for you to love that person?

_____

_____

_____

What would make it easier to love that difficult person?

_____

_____

_____

"Loving and loving behavior are willful choices that we can make with our daily decisions."

*Lord, increase my ability to love and to make loving decisions.* ■

# The Level Ground

**REFLECT**

Consider the "gray" areas of your life. Are there situations where you've built some "good" rationalizations?

_____

_____

_____

**REFLECT**

Return to these areas that you have rationalized. As you think about God's commands, what would He want in the situation?

_____

_____

_____

> **W**e need God's perspective in deciding what is and what is not a "little thing" in our lives.

**1 SAMUEL 2:12–17**
*Now the sons of Eli were corrupt; they did not know the LORD. And the priests' custom with the people was that when any man offered a sacrifice, the priest's servant would come with a three-pronged fleshhook in his hand while the meat was boiling. Then he would thrust it into the pan, or kettle, or cauldron, or pot; and the priest would take for himself all the fleshhook brought up. So they did in Shiloh to all the Israelites who came there.*

*Also, before they burned the fat, the priest's servant would come and say to the man who sacrificed, "Give meat for roasting to the priest, for he will not take boiled meat from you, but raw."*

*And if the man said to him, "They should really burn the fat first; then you may take as much as your heart desires," he would then answer him, "No, but you must give it to me now; and if not, I will take it by force."*

*Therefore the sin of the young men was very great before the LORD, for men abhorred the offering of the LORD.*

**E**li was the next to last judge of Israel and the high priest as well. This righteous man raised Samuel from the time he was weaned. He had a good heart, but he didn't know how to be a father to his sons. They were not men of integrity. The passage says it clearly—"They were corrupt." Perhaps Eli was like so many of us who are busy with work and ministry. After the hours that Eli spent helping others, he just didn't have much time left for his own family.

But rather than emphasize the struggle with our time commitments, let's put ourselves in the place of Eli's two sons and look at their struggle with obedience and integrity. Rather than wait for the people to decide what part of the meat they would give to the priest, they decided to ask for what they wanted. After all, they were the priests.

And the meat would be given to them as a tithe. Why not collect it early? Their request didn't seem like much of a change from God's command.

From a human perspective, it didn't seem like a big thing. From God's perspective, however, "The sin of the young men was very great before the LORD." I'm sure that if we were to talk with these young men about what they were doing, they would have rationalized away most of our concerns. "No big deal!"

Even their father's gentle rebuke (1 Sam. 12:22–25) was ignored, for Eli had long ago lost any meaningful contact with his sons. I suspect that they were raised with an emotionally absent father, who was probably absent for all the "right" reasons.

If we have been wounded by an absent father, either physically or emotionally, we probably also struggle with obedience and integrity. Having had to raise ourselves in terms of what it means to be a man, we've learned to make do. We've gained the skill of rationalizing our behavior so that we've learned how to survive.

One of the signs that we have sufficiently grieved over our woundedness is our desire for integrity even in the little things. Like David, we want to stand on level ground. We've become tired of trying to balance what can't be balanced. Balancing our life always begins with the little things; at least what we consider to be little. For often what seems little to us is big in God's perspective.

*Reveal to me those "little things" that need to be changed in my life, Lord.* ■

**REFLECT**

How can you change your situation so that you are on level ground with God?

_____

_____

_____

**REFLECT**

Spend some time thanking the Lord for His ability to help you change.

_____

_____

_____

> "**Balancing our life always begins with the little things; at least what we consider to be little.**"

# Standing Straight

**Take a 3 x 5 card with you today and keep track of every instance where you bend the truth or hedge things a bit or a lot.**

**Write down some of the things you did that would betray your sense of integrity if others knew about them.**

_____

_____

_____

> **God promises to give us dominion over greater things when we have been faithful in the little things.**

2 CORINTHIANS 4:1–6

*Therefore, since we have this ministry, as we have received mercy, we do not lose heart. But we have renounced the hidden things of shame, not walking in craftiness nor handling the word of God deceitfully, but by manifestation of the truth commending ourselves to every man's conscience in the sight of God.*

*But even if our gospel is veiled, it is veiled to those who are perishing, whose minds the god of this age has blinded, who do not believe, lest the light of the gospel of the glory of Christ, who is the image of God, should shine on them.*

*For we do not preach ourselves, but Christ Jesus the Lord, and ourselves as your servants for Jesus' sake.*

*For it is the God who commanded light to shine out of darkness who has shone in our hearts to give the light of the knowledge of the glory of God in the face of Jesus Christ.*

Doug felt like his world was crashing in. Although he spent long hours at the office, he wasn't getting any encouragement from his supervisor. His children were rapidly growing up. By the time Doug dragged in the front door, exhausted, his small children were already in bed. From the demands of his corporation, Doug spent several weeks a month traveling, and that put even more distance between himself and his family. Each time he returned home, Doug and his family had to adjust to having a father in the house again.

Now it was late at night and he sat in his study at home, going through some random papers from the office. Down the hall, Doug could hear his wife catching the late news on television. As he thought about his life, Doug wondered if there was any way to rescue it and turn it around. There was so much to change and fix in his life that Doug wondered where to begin. How could he have an honest and growing relationship with Christ and his family?

If there was ever someone who should consider giving up, it would be the Apostle Paul. Stoned and beaten for the cause of Christ, Paul continued to travel and preach the Good News about Jesus. In contrast to the rationalizing behavior of Eli's sons, Paul chose not to operate out of a lust for power and control. Keenly aware of the grace and mercy of the living God, Paul knew that God could guide his steps in a different direction. Every day, Paul lived with the awareness that he was functioning on behalf of Christ; Paul was acting as an ambassador for God Himself. He wanted every action that he took to be clear and honest before God and his listeners. Paul wanted to stand on even ground.

What would our lives be like if we could say with Paul, "I have renounced any shameful, deceitful actions on my part. I want every aspect of my life to stand straight both in the sight of others and in the sight of God." How would we be different?

**REFLECT**

List some steps you can take to begin to be careful in the little things.

_____

_____

_____

**REFLECT**

Write out a commitment to yourself to more consistently walk in integrity from this day forward.

_____

_____

_____

" **Paul knew God, because of His grace and mercy, could guide his steps in a different direction.** "

*Lord, it's easy to get discouraged with how far I need to change. Give me Your perspective of love.* ∎

# *B*lessed in Obedience

**REFLECT**

What principles from the life of Caleb can you incorporate into your daily walk with Christ?

_____

_____

_____

**REFLECT**

Describe a situation in which you struggled with being obedient or with maintaining your integrity. It can either be a situation where you failed, or where you succeeded.

_____

_____

_____

> **O**ur ability to stand against the flow is proportional to how much we have internalized the living Word of God.

JOSHUA 14:6–8
*Then the children of Judah came to Joshua in Gilgal. And Caleb the son of Jephunneh the Kenizzite said to him: "You know the word which the LORD said to Moses the man of God concerning you and me in Kadesh Barnea.*

*"I was forty years old when Moses the servant of the LORD sent me from Kadesh Barnea to spy out the land, and I brought back word to him as it was in my heart.*

*"Nevertheless my brethren who went up with me made the heart of the people melt, but I wholly followed the LORD my God."*

**C**aleb was a man of integrity and faith. Forty-five years prior to the events in this passage, Caleb and Joshua stood apart from the rest of Israel by daring to differ with the those who reported that it would be impossible to conquer the land promised to Israel by God. They agreed that the task would be difficult, but they believed it could be done with God's help. Hindsight always makes courageous steps like these seem simple, but we each know how difficult it is to stand up and differ with the majority opinion.

The obedience typified by Caleb is like the obedience described in Psalm 1:1–2, in which the psalmist wrote that those who stop listening to the counsels of evil men will be blessed.

> Blessed is the man
> Who walks not in the counsel of the ungodly,
> Nor stands in the path of sinners,
> Nor sits in the seat of the scornful;
> But his delight is in the law of the LORD,
> And in his law he meditates day and night.

In *The Masculine Journey*, Robert Hicks noted that the man described in Psalm 1 ruled his life by "meditating and listening to the voice of God in Scripture. . . . Because this psalm opens the Psalter, it may be the definitive statement about what the mature man looks like and how you and I may become one!" He also points out that this maturity within our manhood goes well beyond being dependent on the great preachers of our day, on our wives, or on any other outside authority that seeks to influence us. But it does not mean we are self-sufficient. To the contrary, the Psalm clearly states that the authority is the deep scriptural insight we have built over time as we meditate and listen to God's voice in Scripture.

Integrity is built on the internalization and personal application of God's truth as revealed to us in the Bible. We don't just quote the Bible, we live out its truths in our behavior, our attitudes, our brokenness, our sense of powerlessness, and our sensitivity to what breaks the heart of God. We are men who know how to rule our own souls, because we have grieved the wounds and heard the Word of God in a refreshing new way.

When we develop our faithfulness in this way, God is faithful to reward us with what He has promised—a life that is blessed in the deeper ways, not just on the surface.

*I want to stand faithful with You, Lord, day by day. Help me to internalize more of Your Word in my life.* ∎

**REFLECT**

What made the difference between success or failure in that situation? What has typically made it easier for you to be obedient in the past?

_____

_____

_____

**REFLECT**

What are some of the "little" ways in which you need to be more careful about your integrity?

_____

_____

_____

"**We each know how difficult it is to stand up and differ with the majority.**"

# Bending the Truth

**Think of one situation in which you either bent the truth or spoke the brutal truth.**

_____

_____

_____

**REFLECT**

**Describe how you could have spoken the truth in love, edifying and imparting grace to the hearer?**

_____

_____

_____

> **W**e need to develop ears that can hear the hearts of those we love, so we can better speak the truth in love to them.

EPHESIANS 4:25–32

*Therefore, putting away lying, each one speak truth with his neighbor, for we are members of one another.*

*"Be angry, and do not sin"; do not let the sun go down on your wrath nor give place to the devil. Let him who stole steal no longer, but rather let him labor, working with his hands what is good, that he may have something to give him who has need.*

*Let no corrupt communication proceed out of your mouth, but what is good for necessary edification, that it may impart grace to the hearers. And do not grieve the Holy Spirit of God, by whom you were sealed for the day of redemption. Let all bitterness, wrath, anger, clamor, and evil speaking be put away from you, with all malice.*

*And be kind to one another, tenderhearted, forgiving one another, just as God in Christ also forgave you.*

In the third grade, I learned that lying could be a great source of protection. My dad's Irish temper flared at a moment's notice, so I found ways to avoid the truth. Repeatedly, my parents had warned me *not* to walk in the snow banks which were between the sidewalks and the streets. But the snow banks were a fun place to walk! So one day, I was walking through the snow banks on my way home from school—except I slipped into a puddle and came home soaking wet. Immediately I created a story to avoid a trip to the basement with my father. I told how a friend had pushed me into the snow bank and that was how I got wet. If my father had learned that I was lying and actually had gone into the snow bank, I would have been taken to the basement and treated to some licks on my backside with his leather belt. At an early age, I learned how to tell little white lies—they could protect.

In the early days of the church, Ananias and Sapphira thought they could get away with stretching the truth. They sold some property and only brought part of the money to the Apostles. Maybe they had some good plan for what they would do with the extra money. Instead of saying that they had not given the entire amount, they held back part of it and said they had given it all as an offering. The Apostle Peter said to them, "You have not lied to men, but to God" (Acts 5:4). Because they stretched the truth, Ananias and Sapphira both died.

Have you ever bent the truth for good reasons? Have you ever been "brutally" honest? If you reflect for a moment, you know you have probably done both, though one will probably occur more often than the other. Which one do you do the most?

When we bend the truth, we sometimes do it out of concern for the other, but more often we do it to avoid conflict or to save face. Paul gives some criteria in today's passage for how we are to speak the truth: First, we are to speak the truth in love, and second, we are to speak what is good for necessary edification, so that "it may impart grace to the hearers."

Speaking the truth in love requires some sensitivity to the ability of the listener to hear what we have to say. What difficulties do you have in being sensitive to how your listener is hearing what you are saying?

_____

_____

_____

Sometimes we need help in picking up the cues that inform us how the listener is receiving what we have to say. Who in your life could help you learn these cues better? Identify a situation where you will ask that person to help you.

_____

_____

_____

> "Have you ever bent the truth for good reasons?"

*Lord, help me to speak the truth and not to bend it, even a little.* ■

# *Slipping through Cracks*

Who's praying that you will have a good conscience and live honorably? List their names below.

_____

_____

_____

Are you meeting with a group of men who hold you accountable? How could you create one? If you are meeting, how accountable do you feel to them? In what ways could you be more accountable?

_____

_____

_____

> **A** life of obedience is built on the prayers and support of those who know and care about us.

HEBREWS 13:18–19
*Pray for us, for we are confident that we have a good conscience, in all things desiring to live honorably.*
*But I especially urge you to do this, that I may be restored to you the sooner.*

The more we live isolated lives, the more difficult it becomes for us to be obedient. Loners don't usually struggle with issues of integrity or obedience. When there is no one in our lives that really matter to us, what difference does it make anyway? It's not that being a loner causes us to lose our integrity—it's more that as we compromise our values, we withdraw more and more from relationship with other people.

It easy to become anonymous in our world today. The newspapers are filled with bizarre things people do that aren't discovered until some fluke brings their behavior to light. Former CIA Agent Aldrich Ames was sentenced to life in prison for living the double life of a Soviet spy. For years, he had rationalized his selling of U.S. secrets to the Soviets. Only when the government began following Ames's money trail was his double life revealed. For years the government had assumed that his extra income came from the wealthy family of Ames's wife. Up to that point, Ames had managed to live a dual life, and he had escaped attention for years. His anonymous existence carried a heavy price tag—the rest of his life behind bars.

Today we can float between churches, jobs, and even friends, making it easy to be basically unknown by anyone. When we want to make our lives count, the anonymity of individuals in our culture works against us. But when we let our integrity slide, and shade the corners on obedience, anonymity makes it easier to slip through the cracks without anyone really knowing.

The writer of Hebrews didn't want to slip through the cracks and so he asked his readers to pray for him to have a good conscience and "in all things . . .to live honorably."

In my own life, I have a friend who keeps me from being anonymous. My partner in the counseling center and I meet each week to pray for each other. We talk about different areas where we want to grow and then hold each other accountable. He helps me have a measuring stick in my life for prayer and accountability. It can be risky and frightening in some ways to begin such a relationship, but for me it has been vital to my growth.

**REFLECT**

In what ways are you holding the other men in your life accountable?

_____

_____

_____

**REFLECT**

Do you know anyone well enough to really pray that they maintain a good conscience and live honorably? What more would you need to know to be able to do this?

_____

_____

_____

> "When we let our integrity slide, anonymity makes it easier to slip through the cracks."

*Lord, give me the courage to be accountable with at least one other man.* ■

# *The Challenge of Submission*

**REFLECT**

How do you define submission, and what do you expect from your wife in this area?

_____

_____

_____

**REFLECT**

How can you stop demanding the power of submission from your loved ones? List some concrete steps.

_____

_____

_____

**P**art of being manly is knowing how to be submissive.

EPHESIANS 5:18–23

*And do not be drunk with wine, in which is dissipation; but be filled with the Spirit, speaking to one another in psalms and hymns and spiritual songs, singing and making melody in your heart to the Lord, giving thanks always for all things to God the Father in the name of our Lord Jesus Christ, submitting to one another in the fear of God.*

*Wives, submit to your own husbands, as to the Lord. For the husband is head of the wife, as also Christ is head of the church; and He is the Savior of the body.*

**M**ost of us have a pretty good idea what the word *submission* means. Webster says it is "to give over or yield to the power or authority of another." In trying to be more open to the role of women in our lives, many of us have struggled with the concept of how our wives submit. We agree that there needs to be balance, and we don't want them to be doormats. But no matter how hard we try, the word *submission* still means giving someone else some kind of power over another person.

Some years ago I tried to add new meaning to the concept of submission by defining it in the sense of openness, or becoming more transparent as a person. While this may be a valid part of submission, it still doesn't eliminate the "doormat" concept.

Over the years, the words of Paul to the Ephesians have been used to support a kind of macho-masculinity that says, "Wives have to submit, and husbands have to make certain they do." What is missed in that approach is the idea that men are to submit to their wives as well.

It is clear in the passage above. Paul begins this

section by saying that we should be "submitting to one another in the fear of God." Does that just apply to women? Hardly! For later Paul wrote, "Husbands love your wives, just as Christ also loved the church and gave Himself for it."

When you compare your submission to the submission of Christ, it is demanding and costly. It is more than simply giving over the power in your life to someone else. Paul asks husbands to submit to the point of giving their life for their wives.

Have you ever stopped and considered how much Christ loved the Church? More than the Church loved Him, right? Christ was the initiator of love and the Church the receiver. Hasn't Christ done far more for the Church than the Church has ever done for Him, and to this day, Christ continues to meet the needs of the Church, rather than the other way around. That's submission! That's submissive love. And men are given the challenge to love that way.

Let's stop worrying about the amount of submission from our wives. The only person we can directly change is ourselves. Instead, let's increase our concern about how we are doing with our submissive love. Not only is that an important part of what we bring to a marriage, it's an essential part of being a man in today's world.

*God, I want to love my family in a new way. Help me to learn the concept of submission as Christ loves the Church.* ∎

**REFLECT**

Think about how much Christ loves the Church and the sacrifices that He has made through the centuries for her. Write down some that come to mind.

_____

_____

_____

**REFLECT**

What steps can you take to love your wife in a fresh manner and submit to her? List three ideas.

_____

_____

_____

> "**When you compare your submission to the submission of Christ, it is demanding and costly.**"

# Competition or Cooperation?

**How do you find a balance between conceited selfishness, and being too passive and submissive? How do you find the balance between prideful ambition and selfishness, and "putting yourself down?"**

_____

_____

_____

**Which friends or members of your family make it difficult to follow Paul's statement, which encourages us to look out for their interests as well as our own?**

_____

_____

_____

> **D**eeper masculine traits do not include competitiveness. They do include cooperativeness.

PHILIPPIANS 2:1–4

_Therefore if there is any consolation in Christ, if any comfort of love, if any fellowship of the Spirit, if any affection and mercy, fulfill my joy by being likeminded, having the same love, being of one accord, of one mind._

_Let nothing be done through selfish ambition or conceit, but in lowliness of mind let each esteem others better than himself._

_Let each of you look out not only for his own interests, but also for the interests of others._

**A**s a boy I sat in many youth meetings. One of the favorite activities was a "sword drill." In those old-fashioned Bible competitions, the leader called out different verses and we paged through our Bibles as fast as possible to be the first one to reach it. I remember Becky Aldrich. She was practically unbeatable. We boys in the room kind of hung our heads to admit that we had been bested by a girl. But we always got her back during the races out behind the church. Although Becky ran her hardest, one of the boys always crossed the finish line in first place.

One of my friends learned about competition during junior high school. Jimmy sent off for a greeting card sales kit. If he only knocked on enough doors and talked hard enough, he might sell enough boxes of cards to earn a bicycle. He gave it his best shot but he quickly learned that he was not gifted at sales. In comparison to the other junior salesmen in his area, Jimmy came in last place.

What if, instead of knocking on so many doors and talking so much, Jimmy had simply bought the cards and given them away—wouldn't that have been looking out for the interests of others, as the Scripture suggests? Yes, but his parents would have been stuck with a huge bill for cards and Jimmy wouldn't have learned anything about competition in business.

Much of our training as men involves competition. We compete in school, in sports, at work, in our recreation. In many ways, all of life is competitive. Doesn't it seem that if I begin to esteem others as better than myself, when I am better than they are, I live a lie? What does Paul's statement have to do with being a man today? His concept "consider others better than yourself" seems to go counter to everything we've been taught about self-esteem and masculinity.

I don't think Paul was asking us to grovel and act like a lowly person with no self-worth. The context in which he made this statement was to urge us as believers to be "of one accord" and avoid any conceit or selfishness in our relationships. As I examine my relationships with other men, with my family and friends, I need to consider their perspective instead of looking out only for myself.

Why do you think you struggle with these particular people?

_____

_____

How realistic is it that we are to be "like-minded, having the same love, being of one accord, of one mind?" In what situations do you find your behaviors or attitudes at odds with what Paul asks?

_____

_____

_____

"In many ways, all of life is competitive."

*Lord, mold me into someone who looks out for the interests of others.* ∎

# Submitting to Strength

**REFLECT**

In today's competitive business environment, is it possible as a man to be "like-minded," doing nothing "through selfish ambition or conceit"?

_____

_____

_____

**REFLECT**

How do you struggle with finding the balance between pride and self-doubt? Describe an example.

_____

_____

_____

> **Submission is always done properly when it is done in the context of a loving relationship.**

PHILIPPIANS 2:5–8
_Let this mind be in you which was also in Christ Jesus, who, being in the form of God, did not consider it robbery to be equal with God, but made Himself of no reputation, taking the form of a servant, and coming in the likeness of men._

_And being found in appearance as a man, He humbled Himself and became obedient to the point of death, even the death of the cross._

The clearest example of masculine submission in the Bible is described for us in this brief but powerful passage from Paul. It describes how Jesus, in loving the Church, submitted himself to the humiliation, not only of becoming human, but also to the pain of the cross. Whole books have been written on these few verses, for they are rich in content, not only about submission, but other important concepts as well.

An important progression of thought regarding submission that can be found in this passage begins with the "right" that Jesus had to be God. He was and is God. But He chose to empty Himself of His privilege. To go back to our definition of submission, Jesus chose to place Himself under the authority of the Father. But Jesus went beyond that and took on the humbling experience of being in the form of man. Finally, with an obedient spirit, Jesus submitted to death on the cross. That's a powerful example for us as men!

As men, to whom do we submit ourselves? The Bible is clear on this. Paul tells us to submit to the "governing authorities" (Rom. 13:1). This gives us a biblical obligation to obey the rules of government in paying taxes or speed limits. Then, in Ephesians, Paul wrote that we are to "submit to each other," referring to other members of the body of Christ, especially our wives.

Jesus' example of submission removes this concept from the "wimp" category and places it squarely in the context of masculine strength. The easier course of action is to lord your authority over other people. I show real strength of masculine character when I willingly set aside my privileges—including my need to be right, and instead have the mind of Christ in deferring to others.

Now Paul didn't submit so far that he avoided confrontation and always deferred to others. He tried to live a balanced life. Paul felt that Peter was wrong in living a double standard—sometimes Peter would eat with the Gentiles, and other times he did not because he wanted the approval of legalists. Paul didn't ignore the matter but stood up to Peter and confronted him. Jesus also confronted those who were wrong—the money changers, the Pharisees, and other religious leaders. Obviously, submission isn't an attitude of always giving in to others. To have submission in your life, there is a balance between knowing when to act and knowing when to give in to others.

A higher principle governs our decision to submit in any given situation. That principle has to do with both humility and obedience. It also has to do with the valuing of relationship. Jesus submitted to the cross because He loved us. When we as men learn how to value relationships, we will find that masculine balance to submission.

*Thank You, God, for sending Jesus to show us how we should submit to others.* ∎

**REFLECT**

As a man, in what ways do you struggle with the idea of "being submissive?"

_____

_____

_____

**REFLECT**

What "strengths" are you finding as you consider manly submissiveness?

_____

_____

_____

" **Jesus' example of submission places this concept squarely in the context of masculine strength.** "

# *A Lesson in Submission*

> **Submission means that I no longer have to justify myself or my position.**

JOHN 13:3–7

*Jesus, knowing that the Father had given all things into His hands, and that He had come from God and was going to God, rose from supper and laid aside His garments, took a towel and girded Himself.*

*After that, He poured water into a basin and began to wash the disciples' feet, and to wipe them with the towel with which He was girded.*

*Then He came to Simon Peter. And Peter said to Him, "Lord, are You washing my feet?"*

*Jesus answered and said to him, "What I am doing you do not understand now, but you will know after this."*

Take a moment to picture this scene. Because of their pride, not one of the disciples was willing to start the process of foot washing, which was common whenever people came into a house to eat. Usually a slave would perform the task, but with no slave, the host would start the process, and people would participate. Yet this evening, no one was willing to start the process. In fact, they each probably avoided looking at the bowl of water and the towels.

Then Jesus got up and "laid aside His garments, took a towel and girded Himself" to wash the disciples feet. In essence, by girding Himself with a towel, Jesus took on the appearance of a slave. When Peter's turn came, he protested, "You shall never wash my feet!" We can admire Peter for his stand. He knew Jesus was the Christ, the Son of the Living God, and he wasn't going to humiliate Jesus by letting Him wash his feet. That seems reasonable.

But Peter needed to learn to submit to the Lord's plans even when they weren't reasonable, and even when they were the result of Peter's own prideful actions. Submission means I no longer have to justify myself or my position.

Why did Jesus need to take on the role of a servant for His disciples? He says later in the same chapter, "I have given you an example that you should do as I have done to you" (John 13:15).

Several years ago, I learned about the value of submission firsthand. I was going to eliminate my role in a business relationship—provided we could agree on the details. I and several partners met, and the meeting dragged on and on—for four hours. Finally, after I went home, I called the others saying, "I want to forget the entire matter, and I don't need anything out of the business." My tone wasn't angry but submissive to their decision. As a result, the partners got together and offered more money to purchase my share of the business. I could never have predicted such results but they came from my willingness to humbly submit.

 **REFLECT**

In what situations do you have the greatest difficulty acting in a submissive way?

_____

_____

_____

 **REFLECT**

Who is the authority figure in that situation to whom you must submit? Is that person in any way similar to your father or mother? In what ways?

_____

_____

_____

" **By girding Himself with a towel, Jesus took on the appearance of a slave.** "

*Lord, give me opportunities to serve others this week and begin to learn how to submit to others.* ∎

# Genuine Submission

**REFLECT**

**What sort of fears do you have about being a wimp?**

_____

_____

_____

**REFLECT**

**Have you been able to humble your-self in recent situations? Describe them.**

_____

_____

_____

**2 SAMUEL 19:24–28**

*Now Mephibosheth the son of Saul came down to meet the king. And he had not cared for his feet, nor trimmed his mustache, nor washed his clothes, from the day the king departed until the day he came back in peace.*

*So it was, when he had come to Jerusalem to meet the king, that the king said to him, "Why did you not go with me, Mephibosheth?"*

*And he answered, "My lord, O king, my servant deceived me. For your servant said, 'I will saddle a donkey for myself, that I may ride on it and go to the king.' because your servant is lame.*

*"And he has slandered your servant to my lord the king, but my lord the king is like the angel of God. Therefore do what is good in your eyes. For all of my father's house were but dead men before my lord the king. Yet you set your servant among those who eat at your own table. Therefore what right have I still to cry out anymore to the king?"*

> **A submissive attitude can only come from a place of strength.**

The story of Mephibosheth (see also 2 Sam. 16:1–4) is an example of a submissive attitude. Earlier, Mephibosheth had apparently been "deceived" by his servant Ziba. When David was fleeing, Ziba had tricked Mephibosheth in order to deliver food to David and his troops who were fleeing from Absalom. What's more, Ziba told David that Mephibosheth was planning on claiming the kingship, since he was Saul's grandson and last remaining heir.

David didn't have the time to verify Ziba's story. He had to get out of town quickly. Later, when he returned triumphantly, it was Mephibosheth who came to welcome David, not Ziba. During that time, Mephibosheth found out that he had been set up by his servant, and yet he came anyway, with no assurance that David would believe him. For all he knew, David would have had him taken prisoner, or even killed on the spot for his presumed disloyalty. But Mephibosheth came to meet David anyway.

There was a quiet power in Mephibosheth's submission to the king. It was not a manipulative submission, like so much of what we see in our culture today. It was a genuine humbling of Mephibosheth before David that allowed him to say to David, "Do what is good in your eyes."

A few verses later, in reference to a controversy between Mephibosheth and Ziba about land, Mephibosheth's submissive attitude allowed him to say, "Let him (Ziba) take it all." That's genuine submission—to let go of presumed rights in a given situation, because of some higher value or principle that is at work there.

Does this make Mephibosheth a doormat or a wimp? Not at all! If anything, it restored a sense of power and self-control in Mephibosheth's life. The most graphic example of the quiet power in a submissive attitude is seen in Jesus, when He stood before Pilate and his other accusers. When pressed, all Jesus said was, "It is as you say" (Matt. 27:11). As the accusations continued, Jesus was silent. And verse 14 says that Pilate "marveled greatly" at Jesus.

Here is Jesus, the Lord of the universe, who was able with one word to command all of heaven to act on His behalf, willingly submitting to lies and accusations, giving authority to those who either had limited authority or no authority at all. We don't call Jesus a wimp, but on the other hand, we fail to note the quiet, powerful masculine strength exhibited in His submissiveness.

Our fear of being perceived as a wimp has caused us to miss one of the important attitudes that cure the wounds in our masculine soul. We need to discover again the power we can find in submission.

*Lord, submitting takes grace. Help me to discover a large measure of giving and grace.* ∎

**REFLECT**

Is there a Mephibosheth principle that you can apply in your own life today? Is there a situation where you can say, "Let ___ go ahead, I'll wait or I'll do it another time?"

_____

_____

_____

**REFLECT**

Consider situations where you've submitted. How has that situation resulted in an unexpected benefit for you?

_____

_____

_____

"**Genuine submission is letting go of presumed rights because of higher values or principles at work.**"

# *The Paradox*

**REFLECT**

Describe situations in which you were aware of trying too hard to cover up feelings of weakness by appearing strong, and then later feeling as if everyone saw through you.

_____

_____

_____

**REFLECT**

Describe as many examples as you can of situations where less is more and more is less.

_____

_____

_____

> **A** submissive attitude is the place to begin and change.

**MATTHEW 23:8–12**

*"But you, do not be called 'Rabbi'; for One is your Teacher, the Christ, and you are all brethren.*

*"Do not call anyone on earth your father; for One is your Father, He who is in heaven.*

*"And do not be called teachers; for One is your Teacher, the Christ.*

*"But he who is greatest among you shall be your servant.*

*"And whoever exalts himself will be abased, and he who humbles himself will be exalted."*

**J**esus gives us an important insight into masculine submission in this passage. Jesus' paradoxical statement—"Whoever exalts himself will be abased, and he who humbles himself will be exalted"—isn't given as a motivation to be submissive. We don't humble ourselves in order to be exalted. We humble ourselves so that we have the mind of Christ. Jesus was revealing a principle about life that we can live by.

The principle can be stated as "Less is more, and more is less." That may sound like gibberish, but here's how it works. If I seek power *less*, I will be *more* powerful. The *more* I seek power, the *less* real power I will have. The *more* I have a submissive attitude, the *less* I will be perceived as weak; when I am *less* submissive, the *more* I will be perceived as weak.

A more common way to understand this principle is the experience we have all had at sometime where we watch a friend in a situation and say, "I think he's trying too hard." The more he tries, the less we are impressed. Have you ever experienced that with someone?

Shortly after I was married, I felt strongly that I should be the leader in my family life. The church culture almost expects this leadership role from their pastor. The pastor is supposedly in charge of everything—including his home. But underneath I was too scared to know what to do. So I acted as if I were in charge and my wife, Jan, went along with it even though she knew it wasn't right.

One day, Jan came home and said, "I don't care what it is that you are doing, but I want to be God's woman for this situation." That statement rocked my socks. I had to admit that I was trying too hard to lead and impress Jan. And through my admission, I found the strength to change my life. When we don't know and are willing to admit that we don't know, then we begin to open our ears and listen—that's when the strength comes.

**REFLECT**

Describe a situation you are involved in now in which you are either trying too hard or giving up too easily. What could you do that would represent an attitude of humility and manly submissiveness?

_____

_____

_____

"**We don't humble ourselves in order to be exalted. We humble ourselves so that we have the mind of Christ.**"

*Lord, teach me to follow Christ's example of submission.* ∎

# *The Test of Submission*

**REFLECT**

Think about a time when you jumped too quickly out of a submissive attitude.

_____

_____

_____

**REFLECT**

Why did you jump out of that submissive attitude? What caused the jump?

_____

_____

_____

> **A test of my progress will be the growth of a humble and submissive spirit.**

HEBREWS 13:15–17
*Therefore by Him let us continually offer the sacrifice of praise to God, that is, the fruit of our lips, giving thanks to His name.*

*But do not forget to do good and to share, for with such sacrifices God is well pleased.*

*Obey those who rule over you, and be submissive, for they watch out for your souls, as those who must give account. Let them do so with joy and not with grief, for that would be unprofitable for you.*

When we look at the question of submission, we always want to put in qualifiers to our submission to authority figures. "If he were more kind and gracious, it would be easy to submit to his leadership." "If she were more fair, I could submit." But in Scripture, the two are never made conditional upon each other. We don't submit only to benevolent authorities or to passive people.

What is our protection then? What if, in my desire to explore my true masculinity by working on a submissive attitude, I find that others are using me and taking advantage of me? What if, in being submissive to my pastors, they begin to ask me to do more and more at the expense of my family? Even the writer of Hebrews recognizes the danger of a blanket submission when he writes that our leaders should lead "with joy and not with grief, for that would be unprofitable for you."

There is usually a balancing principle in Scripture that creates a tension between one truth and another truth. For example, we are told to be submissive to each other as unto the Lord. But what about the parable of the ten virgins? (See Matthew 25:1–13.) Why weren't the five wise virgins submissive to the needs of the five foolish virgins? When asked for some extra oil for their lamps, the five wise virgins said, "No!" Why weren't they submissive to their sisters?

What about Jesus' instructions regarding reconciliation in Matthew 18? When we have confronted another in the biblical way that Jesus outlines in that chapter and the offending person does not repent, Jesus advises us to "Let him be to you like a heathen and a tax collector."

Obviously, submission in every situation is not going to fulfill what God wants us to experience as men. But having a submissive spirit or attitude is. What's the difference? One is a passive way of relating, whereas a submissive spirit or attitude is an active way of choosing to relate to someone else. It's finding the balance described in Proverbs 22:4, "By humility and the fear of the LORD are riches and honor and life."

As men, our tendency is to jump too quickly out of the submissive attitude and want to either fix the other person or to end the relationship. We need to grow beyond our tendencies, and this can occur as we allow God's healing to penetrate our woundedness. The evidence of His healing work is a growing attitude of humility and submissiveness that still knows how to set limits on abusive or presumptive behaviors. That balance is our goal, and like any balanced position, it isn't easy to find and maintain.

*God, help me to set limits on my abusive behaviors and to grow an attitude of humility.* ∎

REFLECT

Describe some abusive or presumptive behaviors in your life.

_____

_____

_____

REFLECT

Plan a course of action to be more balanced in this area of submission.

_____

_____

_____

"**A submissive spirit or attitude is an active way of choosing to relate to someone else.**"

# *Adaptable, with Limits*

**REFLECT**

How do you handle the unexpected and unpredictable change? In your work? In your family? In your church family?

_____

_____

_____

**REFLECT**

Describe a situation in which you've known that you should rejoice but it looked nearly impossible.

_____

_____

_____

> **G**od's peace is never based on circumstances, only on our submissive attitude coupled with thanksgiving and prayer.

PHILIPPIANS 4:4–9
*Rejoice in the Lord always. Again I will say, rejoice! Let your gentleness be known to all men. The Lord is at hand. Be anxious for nothing, but in everything by prayer and supplication, with thanksgiving, let your requests be made known to God; and the peace of God, which surpasses all understanding, will guard your hearts and minds through Christ Jesus.*

*Finally, brethren, whatever things are true, whatever things are nobel, whatever things are just, whatever things are pure, whatever things are lovely, whatever things are of good report, if there is any virtue and if there is anything praiseworthy—meditate on these things.*

**O**ne of my friends, Mike, had been working on a large business deal for months. Suddenly the people who would make the decisions had cold feet and backed out of the proposal—totally unexpectedly since throughout the time they had been signaling that the project would go ahead. Mike was devastated. Although the factors were outside of his control, his boss didn't understand how Mike was a victim and flailed him with negative messages. Like a turtle in a shell, Mike pulled back in his drive and intensity. After a few months, Mike left the company and took his career into a different direction. The lack of predictability threw him into a tailspin.

Some people are very adaptable by nature, whereas others recoil at the thought of having something start one way and then change directions midway through the process. Neither perspective is wrong. Paul was adaptable. When things didn't go as he planned, he adjusted, but the adaptability of Paul goes beyond personality styles. He had found something that we need.

When we have been wounded in some painful way, we pull back. We become wary of our environment. We lose our ability to adjust to changes, especially those that are unwelcome. The unexpected can set us off into a fit of anger, or a bout with anxiety. We don't like adjusting to the unexpected. We feel secure in predictability.

Our struggle is often intensified by the belief systems we have based on Scriptures like "Rejoice in the Lord always" and "Be anxious for nothing." We know what we should be able to do, but somehow we fail to do it when the situation confronts us. That struggle is often an indicator that we haven't finished healing in some wounded part of our soul.

What were Paul's wounds? One of them had to have been the realization of what he had done in his anger to the Christian church and to Stephen. When did he experience healing of that wound? Probably during the years he spent in preparation for his ministry (See Gal. 1:13ff). And the evidence of his healing is in his ability to be content regardless of the circumstances. His emphasis on rejoicing is even more amazing when we realize that he was writing this to the Philippians from a prison cell.

What was his secret? It begins with what we looked at last week—a humble spirit. Then we add to that an attitude of thanksgiving that covers everything—both welcomed events and dreaded events. Then wrap all this up in prayer. The outcome is God's incredible peace residing within us. God's peace is never based on circumstances, only on our submissive attitude coupled with thanksgiving and prayer. That's what makes an adaptable spirit.

*Lord, help me to combine humbleness with thankfulness in my day.* ■

**REFLECT**

What turned that seemingly impossible situation around? (Often, a task or circumstance initially looks impossible, but after a day or a week, the perspective is different.)

_____
_____
_____

**REFLECT**

What steps can you take to acquire a more humble spirit?

_____
_____
_____

" **Giving thanks in all things opens us to God's perspective and to His unsurpassable peace.** "

# Consistent Contentment

**REFLECT**

On a scale of 1 to 10, with 1 being very discontent and 10 being very content, where would you rate yourself?

☹———————————————☺

1  2  3  4  5  6  7  8  9  10

**REFLECT**

Describe how you experience discontent. Is it a restlessness? A short fuse? A need to be critical? Or . . . ?

_____

_____

_____

> **W**e learn contentment as we practice the right principles.

PHILIPPIANS 4:10–17

*But I rejoiced in the Lord greatly that now at last your care for me has flourished again; though you surely did care, but you lacked opportunity.*

*Not that I speak in regard to need, for I have learned in whatever state I am, to be content; I know how to be abased, and I know how to abound. Everywhere and in all things I have learned both to be full and to be hungry, both to abound and to suffer need.*

*I can do all things through Christ who strengthens me.*

*Nevertheless you have done well that you shared in my distress.*

*Now you Philippians know also that in the beginning of the gospel, when I departed from Macedonia, no church shared with me concerning giving and receiving but you only.*

*For even in Thessalonica you sent aid once and again for my necessities.*

**A**n adaptable spirit is not based on having all our needs met, nor is it only possible when things are going well for us. Paul spoke of being abased, of being hungry, and of being in need. His contentment was consistent in whatever state he was in. And Paul knew variety in the different situations from his life.

As he traveled throughout Asia Minor preaching the Good News about Jesus, Paul met with opposition—sometimes the crowd threw him out of the town and other times they stoned him. Once the people left Paul "for dead" but he got up and went to his friends, nursed his wounds and continued. Sometimes he didn't know anyone in a particular area, so he worked his craft as a tentmaker. Many of his letters were written in prison and he was even shipwrecked. In the final chapter of Acts, Paul crawled onto the shore after he was shipwrecked and then a deadly snake bit him. The people of the island sat and watched to see if Paul would die. When Paul didn't become ill, they said he was god. Talk about extremes of situations—death sentenced prisoner to god-like stature.

Some of our common images of masculinity are built around a certain stoicism. Many of those images from television or movies perpetuate our culture. Curled up in our easy chair, we've watched the Lone Ranger repeatedly riding off into the sunset. Or in the final scene of a John Wayne movie, he leaves the woman behind that he loves because cowboys are loners and would rather spend time out with their horses on the open plains. Raised with these images, we believe that manliness is found in our isolated contentment. We suffer simply because that is the manly thing to do. That's not what Paul was describing. He was talking about a contentment supported by relationships, about people who cared and supported him, sending aid once and again for his necessities. The fellowship with other men and the relationships from the churches kept Paul going. He discovered a great joy through giving and receiving from others.

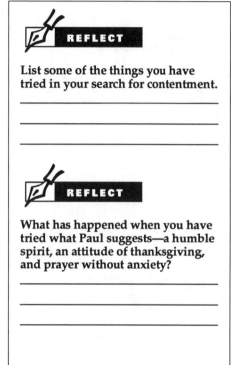

**REFLECT**

List some of the things you have tried in your search for contentment.

_____

_____

_____

**REFLECT**

What has happened when you have tried what Paul suggests—a humble spirit, an attitude of thanksgiving, and prayer without anxiety?

_____

_____

_____

> "We suffer simply because that is the manly thing to do."

*Lord, help me find the relationships with other men that will keep me content despite my circumstances.* ∎

# More than Workaholics

**REFLECT**

Think about the life of Paul and how you can learn from his example. What is your main purpose in life or your driving force?

_____

_____

_____

**REFLECT**

Are you working in the context of relationships or alone? What steps can you take today to strengthen your relationships?

_____

_____

_____

> **T**o become adaptable, we need to look to the life of Paul as a role model for us.

2 CORINTHIANS 4:13–18

_But since we have the same spirit of faith, according to what is written, "I believed and therefore I spoke," we also believe and therefore speak, knowing that He who raised up the Lord Jesus will also raise us up with Jesus, and will present us with you. For all things are for your sakes, that grace, having spread through the many, many cause thanksgiving to abound to the glory of God._

_Therefore we do not lose heart. Even though our outward man is perishing, yet the inward man is being renewed day by day._

_For our light affliction, which is but for a moment, is working for us a far more exceeding and eternal weight of glory, while we do not look at the things which are seen, but at the things which are not seen. For the things which are seen are temporary, but the things which are not seen are eternal._

**P**aul was obviously no stranger to trouble. If you read 2 Corinthians 4, he describes some of the things he had been through over the years. It almost reads like a mini-review of the book of Acts. Then he says, "All things are for your sakes." How can he say that? Is he saying the same thing that some teachers want us to believe: that we are to be thankful _for_ every bad thing that happens in our lives? Are we to be so adaptable that we just bend with everything? That doesn't seem like the manly thing to do!

Paul was obviously a driven man. He had one purpose in his life and that was to make Christ known where He was not known. He traveled extensively with that one purpose as his driving force. How was he different from those of us who are driven to work long hours for our family's benefit?

First, he never sacrificed relationships for the sake of work. Everything he did was in the context of relationships. He was always traveling with someone as his co-worker. He wrote letters to the churches he started, keeping touch with the people, naming them by name on the pages of Scripture. He stopped to see them on his journeys. Paul was not an isolated loner out there working long hours for the sake of the gospel. Relationships were a primary part of his life and work.

Second, he had an over-arching purpose that governed everything he did! Paul wanted to preach Christ and Him crucified. He was driven, but Paul was purposeful in his drive. His purpose was not to have the biggest church, or be the most successful. In fact, he didn't keep score in the human realm; he kept his focus on the "eternal weight of glory." That's why he could say that all his accomplishments were worthless apart from knowing Christ (see Phil. 3:1–10).

Third, Paul never gave up. "We do not lose heart," he told the Corinthians. And Paul was an example of not losing heart—even when he was in prison. Everything was seen as an opportunity, and he approached it with an expectancy that made him open to what God wanted to do within any situation.

Finally, Paul must have been a good listener, for he responded to people problems, criticism, and misunderstandings in great detail. He cared about what others were going through, and he listened enough so that he knew what they were going through. His letters are not a superficial "pat on the head." They represent deep thought and deep empathy.

*Lord, sometimes I do lose heart, but help me to remain focused on You.* ∎

**REFLECT**

When difficulties come, do you face them as opportunities or as problems? Think about your week ahead and how you can face a problem as an opportunity.

_____

_____

_____

**REFLECT**

Are you a good listener? What can you do today to become a good listener and care about the concerns of others?

_____

_____

_____

"**Paul never sacrificed relationships for the sake of work.**"

# *Constant Monitoring*

**REFLECT**

We all believe we operate in the context of sound principles, but what principles really guide your life? How do you decide what you will do and what you won't do? List them.

_____

_____

_____

**REFLECT**

The passage in Proverbs suggest three areas of concern; our mouth, our eyes, and our feet. How do your principles affect these three parts of you?

_____

_____

_____

> **"A prudent man foresees evil and hides himself" (Proverbs 22:3).**

PROVERBS 4:23–27
*Keep your heart with all diligence,*
*For out of it spring the issues of life.*
*Put away from you a deceitful mouth,*
*And put perverse lips far from you.*
*Let your eyes look straight ahead,*
*And your eyelids look right before you.*
*Ponder the path of your feet,*
*And let all your ways be established.*
*Do not turn to the right or the left;*
*Remove your foot from evil.*

**S**ometimes I wonder where one day ends and the another begins. Time seems to be in endless motion. As a therapist, I maintain a private practice, plus I run a private clinic. I'm a partner in another clinic and have a daily radio program. About two weekends per month I speak at some place around the country, and somewhere I squeeze in some time for writing. All of these aspects of my life aren't drudgery. They're something I enjoy.

My big problem is when someone will call me and want an appointment during my already crowded schedule. I'll listen to the concerns of this person and believe I can help, so I'll schedule another one-hour appointment. What gets squeezed? The only two items in my routine with any sort of flexibility—family and fun. Controlling my schedule is a constant battle. I have to work hard at saying "no" and referring the needy people on to other therapists. My wife keeps me accountable in terms of my weekend speaking. Often I wish that time was something I could simply take care of once and for all, but it doesn't work that way. One of my areas of weakness is that I don't acknowledge the pressure on me until almost too late. Then my wife will sit down and remind me that I need to stay ahead of it and keep adaptable.

I've learned that adaptability has its limits. If we are going to avoid being pushed every which way by the circumstances of life, we need to know how to set limits. We need to know how to say "no" to some things and "yes" to other things.

Paul set limits in his life. It is likely that there were other demands on his time and other "good" things that he could have done with his life. It was a likely temptation for Paul to stay in one location and not to move on in his journeys. But he probably set his goals based on his calling to "preach Christ." His principles helped him determine what to do and what not to do. And of course, he was sensitive to God's leading, for sometimes God had something totally different in mind for him, like when he went to Macedonia.

 **REFLECT**

Where have you had the most problems staying focused—your mouth, your eyes, or your feet? Describe some of your struggle.

_____

_____

_____

 **REFLECT**

What are some changes you can begin to make this week to "keep your heart with all diligence"?

_____

_____

_____

> "If we are going to avoid being pushed every which way, we need to know how to set limits."

*Lord, help me to set my priorities according to Your principles and Your will for my life.* ∎

# Setting Limits

**What are the fences that you have set in your life?**

_____

_____

_____

**Describe two opportunities that you've turned down in the last week.**

_____

_____

_____

> **Learning how to set limits in our lives is an important part of our development as a person and as a man.**

MATTHEW 25:1–5

_"Then the kingdom of heaven shall be likened to ten virgins who took their lamps and went out to meet the bridegroom._

_"Now five of them were wise, and five were foolish._

_"Those who were foolish took their lamps and took no oil with them, but the wise took oil in their vessels with their lamps._

_"But while the bridegroom was delayed, they all slumbered and slept."_

Learning how to set limits in our lives is an important part of our development as a person and as a man.

Setting limits is not an automatic process within us, especially if we have been wounded by our father. The absence of a father or the abuse of a father leaves our ability to set limits up in the air.

Saying no is not easy for many of us, especially when it means we have to say no to things that aren't really bad. We often think that if we say no to someone, we are acting selfishly. Sometimes we have been taught that saying no is unspiritual; that those who are eager to follow the Lord will take advantage of every opportunity presented to them. What we overlook is that there are generally two types of people we are going to relate to—those who act responsibly and those who act irresponsibly. Saying yes to irresponsible behavior is encouraging sinful patterns.

Today, take the time to read the entire parable of the wise and the foolish virgins (Matt. 25:1–13). The wise virgins were responsible. Jesus said they came prepared with extra oil for their lamps in case the bridegroom was delayed in his coming. But the foolish virgins acted irresponsibly. They came unprepared and thought that someone else would be responsible for their oversight. The way Jesus told the parable makes it very clear that saying no in certain situations can be a very responsible behavior. In fact, it is the one thing that can balance our adaptable spirit so that it doesn't just flex and bend to accommodate anyone. Healthy attitudes of adaptability require us to know when to say no and to have the ability and the freedom to say it.

The point of the parable is Jesus urging us to be ready for His coming, but an important sub-point is our right to say no. When the foolish virgins ran out of oil, they asked the wise virgins for some of their oil. The wise virgins told them that there was not enough oil to share with the foolish virgins. So the foolish virgins had to leave their watch to buy more oil. They missed the arrival of the bridegroom.

It was okay for the wise virgins to refuse the request of the foolish ones. It is not selfish or unspiritual to say no. In fact, our yes is only meaningful when we know how to say no as well.

Think of your no as a fence or a property line. Without these lines, we would be in real trouble trying to define what is ours and what isn't. The same is true personally. When we can't say no, we are going to have a very difficult time defining what is me and what isn't me. Healing for wounded souls requires not only knowing who we are before God, but who we are not as well.

**REFLECT**

As you consider how you have set limits, what have you been able to accomplish as a result?

_____

_____

_____

**REFLECT**

How has setting limits helped you keep in the good and keep out the evil in your life?

_____

_____

_____

"**Setting limits is not automatic, especially if we have been wounded by our father.**"

*God, teach me how to set limits.* ■

# *Just Say No*

**REFLECT**

Think about your friends. Do some of them have immoral values?

_____

_____

_____

**REFLECT**

How are the values of these friends having a bad effect on you morally or spiritually?

_____

_____

_____

**B**ehaving as a man of God will require that we learn to say no to certain people and certain things.

PSALM 101:1–5

*I will sing of mercy and justice;*
*To you, O Lord, I will sing praises.*
*I will behave wisely in a perfect way.*
*Oh, when will You come to me?*
*I will walk within my house with a perfect heart.*
*I will set nothing wicked before my eyes;*
*I hate the work of those who fall away;*
*It shall not cling to me.*
*A perverse heart shall depart from me;*
*I will not know wickedness.*
*Whoever secretly slanders his neighbor,*
*Him I will destroy;*
*The one who has a haughty look and a proud heart,*
*Him I will not endure.*

**D**avid had to learn to say no. As the king of Israel, David had more than one wife. Multiple marriages were common and as the leader of the nation, he could always pick another wife. But David also was responsible to lead the Israelites in God's Laws.

One evening David was walking out on the roof of his palace and looked down. He saw a beautiful woman, Bathsheba, taking a bath. Rather than having the strength to look away, he lusted after her. David's inability to say no had serious consequences. The king brought Bathsheba into his palace and had sex with her. He tried to cover up his mistake by bringing Bathsheba's husband, Uriah, back from the battlefield, and encouraged him to go home to Bathsheba. But David's plan failed. Ultimately, David sent Uriah back to the battlefield and moved him to the front lines so that he was killed in battle. When Bathsheba had David's child, the child became ill and died.

David's inability to say no to his lust for Bathsheba led to serious difficulties both for him and his family. Perhaps the principles he describes in this psalm grew out of his struggle with his sin and the effect that sin had on others. As he begins the psalm, he makes a point of how he needs God's help, especially in living blamelessly within his own home.

The things David vows to avoid in his life are things we need to avoid as well: wickedness, perversion, slander, pride, deceitfulness, and evildoers. David wants nothing to do with any of these, or with people who are comfortable with these things. He says very clearly in verse 7 that they "shall not dwell within my house; . . . shall not continue in my presence." He wants to be with the "faithful of the land."

A constant theme throughout this psalm is the effect other people have on us. The types of people that we allow into our lives can have a large effect for good or for evil.

 **REFLECT**

What are some of the practices going on around you that you need to stay clear of in order to live as a godly man?

_____

_____

_____

 **REFLECT**

Which friends have a good effect on you? How do they do so?

_____

_____

_____

> "A perverse heart shall depart from me."

*Lord, guide my steps and teach me to set limits.* ■

# Caring Enough to Confront

**REFLECT**

What has happened when you have confronted someone?

_____

_____

_____

**REFLECT**

Describe some of the principles that *actually* guide you in your marriage, your family, your work, and your ministry. Locate some other man so you can hold each other accountable in the practicality of the principles you describe.

_____

_____

_____

> **I**f we are going to experience healing within our souls, we need to be in mutually accountable relationships with other men.

1 CORINTHIANS 5:9–13

*I wrote to you in my epistle not to keep company with sexually immoral people.*

*Yet I certainly did not mean with the sexually immoral people of this world, or with the covetous, or extortioners, or idolaters, since then you would need to go out of the world.*

*But now I have written to you not to keep company with anyone named a brother, who is a fornicator, or covetous, or an idolater, or a reviler, or a drunkard, or an extortioner—even to eat with such a person.*

*For what have I to do with judging those also who are outside? Do you not judge those who are inside?*

*But those who are outside God judges. Therefore "put away from yourselves that wicked person."*

**A** part of setting limits as Christians is that we are to hold each other accountable. All too often, our energy is spent in trying to clean up the act of those who are not believers. In this passage, Paul encourages the Corinthians to keep close accounts with each other within the family of faith.

How do we do that without being judgmental? Obviously, it is built on relationship. There has to be some history of caring, concern, trust, and integrity. There also has to be a sense of mutuality, where we hold others accountable, and they hold us accountable.

I've talked recently to two women whose husbands left them for another woman. In both situations, the couple was very involved within the church, and in both cases, the husband was involved with a support group within the church. Neither husband was held accountable by the men he was meeting with. One of them continued on in the support group after he had left his wife and "went public" with his wife-to-be.

If we are going to experience healing within our

souls, we need to be in mutually accountable relationships with other men. I don't know if the outcome might have been different if these two men were in groups with mutual accountability. But I am certain that for the other men in the group there would have been growth and healing within them if they had been attempting to hold the other two accountable.

It takes courage to confront a friend who is slipping into some destructive behavior pattern. But if we are going to be God's men, we need to find that courage. And we must care enough about each other to not only agree to hold each other accountable, but to confront.

David Augsberger, in his book, *Caring Enough to Confront*, calls it "care-fronting." Its motivation is not judgment, it is caring and love. That means we have friends in our lives who know us well enough to be able to care, and they know us well enough to know what to confront.

I don't gain any personal joy from confrontation. To confront another man has to be approached with great thought and care. Sometimes when I risk a confrontation, it could end the relationship. I can't control the response of the other person but I can control my words of care and my look of concern and compassion. Each time I risk and confront another brother, I need to make sure that it is built on a solid relationship.

 **REFLECT**

To whom are you accountable?

_____

_____

_____

 **REFLECT**

How comfortable are you being accountable to a group?

_____

_____

_____

> **"The motivation for mutual accountability is not judgment. It is caring and love."**

*Lord, teach me to keep close accounts with the men in my life.* ■

# The Context for Healing

**REFLECT**

Think about your close friends. List two below.

_____

_____

_____

**REFLECT**

How could you encourage these friends today? There is truth to the saying that "he who would have friends must be friendly."

_____

_____

_____

**1 SAMUEL 18:1–4**

*And it was so, when he had finished speaking to Saul, that the soul of Jonathan was knit to the soul of David, and Jonathan loved him as his own soul.*

*Saul took him that day, and would not let him go home to his father's house anymore.*

*Then Jonathan and David made a covenant, because he loved him as his own soul.*

*And Jonathan took off the robe that was on him and gave it to David, with his armor, even to his sword and his bow and his belt.*

**T**o become God's man, we need to be in relationships, including lasting friendships with other men.

**O**ne of the deepest friendships recorded in the Bible is that of Jonathan and David. Although Jonathan was probably older than David, they hit it off right from the beginning. A deep love and attachment grew between them that reflected their commitment to God. It was stronger than even their commitment to their own families. Jonathan showed this through his protection of David when Saul was trying to kill David. Even when Jonathan found out that David was to be the next king instead of him, their friendship was strengthened.

Few of us have friends like that. Friendship is not typically something sought by or held on to by men. Most of our friends are the husbands of our wife's friends, or someone we spend time with only at work, or someone whose son is on our son's little league team. In other words, our friends are usually other men with whom we relate to indirectly, through someone or something other than simply friendship.

A lot of subtle pressures in our culture work against our having friends. We have the competitive pressures of work that demand our time. We feel guilty if we take time away from our families, especially since we are probably under pressure to spend more time there. We move from city to city, and we often don't take the time to keep up on old friendships, so they are easily lost through distance and the passing of time.

The death rate of single men is twice that of married men and three times that of single women. The difference is usually explained by the fact that married men at least have a wife and family to relate to, and that single women have lots of friends involved in their lives. Single men are like most men, except more so. They live isolated lives. Obviously, friends are valuable for more than just our physical health, but it seems that having friendships can play a significant role in our physical well-being.

God has created us for relationships. God Himself exists within relationship in the form of the Trinity: Father, Son, and Holy Spirit are constantly in close contact with each other. When God created the world, the only thing in all creation that wasn't good was that man was alone. Whenever we find ourselves alone, we can be certain that, according to God's design for us, it still isn't good. We need relationship and we need friendship. They are part of God's plan.

*God, help me to develop one close male friend.* ■

**REFLECT**

Consider some friends from your past—maybe in a different town. How can you renew your contact with them through a phone call or a letter? Make a plan to do that today.

_____

_____

_____

**REFLECT**

Consider the special friendship that David had with Jonathan. How could you build that type of friendship with one other man?

_____

_____

_____

> **"It seems that having friendships can play a significant role in our physical well-being."**

# *An Unusual Friendship*

**REFLECT**

What kind of friends do you have? Make a list of men whom you would consider to be friends.

_____

_____

_____

**REFLECT**

Go back over your list and put an asterisk by those you could genuinely count on in tough situations, men who would be willing to make personal sacrifices on your behalf. Then make a note of how long each man has been your friend.

_____

_____

_____

> **O**ur ability to know ourselves is expanded by our openness with those who have known us over time.

1 SAMUEL 19:1–2, 4–7

*Now Saul spoke to Jonathan his son and to all his servants, that they should kill David; but Jonathan, Saul's son, delighted much in David.*

*So Jonathan told David, saying, "My father Saul seeks to kill you. Therefore please be on your guard until morning, and stay in a secret place and hide. . . ."*

*Now Jonathan spoke well of David to Saul his father, and said to him, "Let not the king sin against his servant, against David, because he has not sinned against you, and because his works have been very good toward you. . . ." Why then will you sin against innocent blood, to kill David without a cause?"*

*So Saul heeded the voice of Jonathan, and Saul swore, "As the LORD lives, he shall not be killed."*

*Then Jonathan called David, and Jonathan told him all these things. So Jonathan brought David to Saul, and he was in his presence as in times past.*

**S**aul became obsessed with killing David. There were times when he was rational, and David felt safe around Saul, but the majority of the time, Saul was intent on ending David's life. Several times he insisted that Jonathan either kill David himself, or bring him to his father so that he could kill him. Each time, Jonathan not only diplomatically avoided doing what his father asked him to do, he was also able to warn David of the impending danger.

Because of his friendship with David, Jonathan was willing to even disobey his father, the king. There was a maturity in Jonathan's decision. It was reflected in his ability to go against his father's wishes and maintain his sense of self-control. He acted not out of rebellion, but out of principle. Jonathan's obedience was to God first, and then to his friend.

In my own life there are three guys that I consider

close friends. With one of these men, I've been friends since college. During one of the darkest periods of my life, this friendship made an incredible difference in my life. This man was always there to listen and help me sort out the truth from the fiction in my circumstances.

Another one of these three friends took an amazing step of courage recently. He invited myself along with two other friends to meet and discuss three things that he did well and three things that he needed to improve. We took an hour to talk about these different aspects of his life. He didn't put us off, but carefully listened to the joys and concerns. At the end of the session, we laid hands on him and prayed for his life. This experience built amazing depth to our friendship. And if you have the courage, the same experience can happen in your life.

**REFLECT**

**Keeping in touch with boyhood friends gives us a sense of continuity in our lives. As you reflect on your boyhood experiences and friends, which of them could you still contact today? It may be helpful for you in your journey to find several of your "lost" boyhood friends and reestablish contact with them. Write out what you will do to contact them.**

_____

_____

_____

> **"During one of the darkest periods of my life, a friendship made an incredible difference."**

*Thank You, Lord, for friends. Help me to be a friend.* ■

# *A* Wise Friend

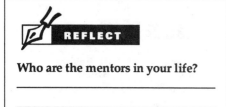

**REFLECT**

Who are the mentors in your life?

_____

_____

_____

**REFLECT**

Who have been your spiritual mentors? Who is your present spiritual mentor?

_____

_____

_____

> **W**e need wise friends who can help us see our blind spots and help us see beyond our near-sightedness.

1 KINGS 19:19–21

*So he departed from there, and found Elisha the son of Shaphat, who was plowing with twelve yoke of oxen before him, and he was with the twelfth. Then Elijah passed by him and threw his mantle on him.*

*And he left the oxen and ran after Elijah, and said, "Please let me kiss my father and my mother, and then I will follow you." And he said to him, "Go back again, for what have I done to you?"*

*So Elisha turned back from him, and took a yoke of oxen and slaughtered them and boiled their flesh, using the oxen's equipment, and gave it to the people, and they ate. Then he arose and followed Elijah, and served him.*

**O**ne type of friendship we find between men in the Bible is a mentor relationship. After Elijah left the cave where he had been hiding in the Sinai, God told him to return to the Wilderness of Damascus and anoint Elisha as his successor. The remainder of Elijah's life was spent mentoring Elisha, and one of the interesting consequences in Elijah's life was a renewed sense of boldness.

Mentors are often seen as father substitutes, and in such cases, the mentoring relationship can be just as disappointing as our relationship with our father. We find a supervisor at work whom we enjoy working with and find the time working with them as a team to be very instructional. But when a promotion comes for ourselves or our supervisor, the relationship all too often ends, and we come away from it with a great deal of disappointment. We thought the friendship went beyond the work.

Sometimes we give up on the relationship. Other times we are rebuffed in some way and back away, aware of the fact that we expected too much. In some of the books written to men, writers warn the readers to be wary when it comes to looking for a mentor. They believe it will always end up in disappointment.

Perhaps that is the case, but when we look at Elisha and Elijah's relationship, it is certainly one of mentoring, and, in their case, Elisha (the younger one) is persistent. He is aggressive and won't let Elijah off the hook. Elisha is very clear about what he wants from the relationship—a double portion of the blessing that Elijah had from God.

The fourth-century church father Basil told his followers to find someone "who may serve you as a very sure guide in the work of leading a holy life." He urged them to find someone who knew the "straight road to God." Augustine agreed, saying that "no one can walk without a guide."

That may go counter to our cultural stereotype of masculinity, which says "I can do it myself." But then much of what God wants us to know and learn goes counter to public opinion.

The story is told of King Henry III of Bavaria, who reigned in the eleventh century. He grew tired of the pressures of being king and applied to join a nearby monastery. The prior, a friend of his, was a bit incredulous and asked the king if he knew that, as a monk, he would have to obey in everything he was told to do. It's easy to imagine the king's displeasure at his friend's lack of interest. When King Henry answered yes, that he knew and was willing, the prior told him to go back to his throne and serve faithfully in the place God had put him. Although it wasn't what he expected to hear, it was what he needed to hear, and only a friend could help him at that point.

*Lord, show me the mentors in my life who can teach me more about You.* ∎

**REFLECT**

If you don't have a mentor, how could you find one? Someone at church in a place of leadership? Someone in your work place?

_____

_____

_____

**REFLECT**

Have you expressed appreciation for your mentors? Take a minute and drop them a brief note of thanks.

_____

_____

_____

"**Find someone who may serve you as a very sure guide in the work of leading a holy life.**"

# *Mentors and Students*

Think back over your years and identify those who have served as mentors in your life. Think of teachers or friends who helped you learn something, either about yourself or about life, which was important to your growth.

_____

_____

_____

**REFLECT**

Recall some relationships in your past where your expectations exceeded the reality. What did you do? Did you withdraw or press for more?

_____

_____

_____

> **W**hen we remain alone, we are like a burning coal that is isolated. It can only grow cold. We need wise friends to help us see beyond ourselves.

**2 KINGS 2:8–11**
*Now Elijah took his mantle, rolled it up, and struck the water; and it was divided this way and that, so that the two of them crossed over on dry ground.*

*And so it was, when they had crossed over, that Elijah said to Elisha, "Ask! What may I do for you, before I am taken away from you?" And Elisha said, "Please let a double portion of your spirit be upon me."*

*So he said, "You have asked a hard thing. Nevertheless, if you see me when I am taken from you, it shall be so for you; but if not, it shall not be so."*

*Then it happened, as they continued on and talked, that suddenly a chariot of fire appeared with horses of fire, and separated the two of them; and Elijah went up by a whirlwind into heaven.*

In looking at the relationship between Elijah and Elisha, one point stands out. To succeed, the student needs to be the driving force in the relationship. Elijah almost appeared to be passive, acting as though he didn't really care whether Elisha tagged along or not. But Elijah was involved; he simply left the initiative to Elisha.

Proverbs tells us that "As iron sharpens iron, so a man sharpens the countenance of his friend" (27:17). Elijah's superficial lack of interest could have discouraged Elisha, but it didn't. It only served to make him more determined. Both men knew that Elijah would soon be taken into heaven through a whirlwind. So Elisha insisted on traveling with his mentor and they walked from Gilgal to Bethel. Some sons of prophets came out and asked Elisha if he knew that his master would be leaving today. "Yes," Elisha told these sons of prophets. He insisted on traveling with Elijah so that he would see his master be taken into heaven.

For Elisha, it must have been a frightening sight to see a fiery chariot with horses descend from the sky and take up Elijah. Elisha's first action was to grieve the loss of his mentor—he tore his clothes into two pieces. Elijah's mantle was left on the ground, indicating that Elisha's request to receive a double portion of Elijah's spirit had been granted. He walked back to the river and struck it with the water and it instantly divided. From observation and from first-hand experience, Elisha learned from his mentor. In a very real sense, one of Elijah's greatest contributions was his mentoring of Elisha.

Early on in my ministry a pastor from another church helped me with my priorities. We played basketball together once a week. From my training, I had gathered some warped ideas. Ministry was my top priority, I had been told. This friend helped mentor me and teach me the importance of family, and how it should play a higher part in my life than ministry. Now, more than twenty-five years later, I hardly see him but I appreciate that strong role that he took in my life at a critical point. Mentors who have gained wisdom from experience can help us maneuver the bends in life's road.

**In what ways did your disappointed expectations keep you from being open to others?**

_____

_____

_____

**A mentoring relationship goes beyond a support group or an accountability group. It involves a closer friendship with one person. List some of the ways in which you think a spiritual friend or guide could help you.**

_____

_____

_____

> **"As iron sharpens iron, so a man sharpens the countenance of his friend."**

_Lord, guide my steps to wise men who can mentor different aspects of my life._ ■

# God Works Through Friends

**Consider Timothy and Paul. What risks did Paul take to bring Timothy with him?**

_____

_____

_____

**Friendship involves risk. Consider some risks that your close friends took with you. Describe two of them.**

_____

_____

_____

ACTS 16:1–5

_Then he came to Derbe and Lystra. And behold, a certain disciple was there, named Timothy, the son of a certain Jewish woman who believed, but his father was Greek. He was well spoken of by the brethren who were at Lystra and Iconium._

_Paul wanted him to go on with him. And he took him and circumcised him because of the Jews who were in that region, for they all knew that his father was Greek._

_And as they went through the cities, they delivered to them the decrees to keep, and which were determined by the apostles and elders at Jerusalem. So the churches were strengthened in the faith, and increased in number daily._

**P**aul loved to work within the context of his friendships. He traveled with Barnabas, with Luke, with Silas, with John Mark, and with others. Some worked out nicely, while others, like his early trip with John Mark, were disappointing.

One of the men he took with him was Timothy, a young man with a growing reputation. In this situation, Paul, the mentor, was the moving force behind their relationship. Timothy was obviously willing, for he allowed himself to be circumcised before they left. He apparently traveled with Paul on both his second and third missionary trips, setting up churches, facing opposition and prison, and, all in all, spending time with Paul and learning from him.

Timothy had a Jewish mother and a Gentile father. His mixed racial background probably led to tensions, and to his timid nature. He certainly wasn't a brash Elisha who would ask for double of everything. He wouldn't have even

> **S**ometimes our relationships are based on our initiative; sometimes it takes the initiative of the other person to get it started.

thought of asking Paul if he could go with him on his travels. It took the wisdom and confidence of Paul to press the point home to Timothy. Paul saw great potential in this young man.

Paul's relationship with Timothy was not a short-lived one. Paul sent him to Corinth to deal with some of the problems there. (See 1 Cor. 4:1.) He left Timothy in Ephesus to oversee the church there. Paul kept in touch with Timothy over the years and near the end of his life, Paul wrote two letters to Timothy that are preserved for us in the New Testament.

Sometimes our relationships are based on our initiative; sometimes it takes the initiative of the other person. But in either case there is a responsiveness to friendship that allows God to accomplish His purposes, not only in our lives, but in larger ways as well. Timothy is part of the "we" mentioned at the beginning of five books in the New Testament, and at the end of Hebrews, 1 Corinthians, and Romans. That's quite a legacy for someone who liked to slip into the background.

In our journey towards godly manhood, we have been confronting parts of our life that aren't easy to face. Like Timothy, we could easily want to give up. Yet when we have someone who believes in us, just as Timothy did, we are able to go far beyond what we would normally do, and impact others in the process as well. Before he could leave on the journey with Paul, Timothy had to endure the pain of circumcision. Painful situations are usually doorways to great opportunities, especially where God is concerned. But God usually works through people, so we need to be open to those who believe in us, even when we are filled with self-doubt.

*Lord, help me to find the Pauls and Timothys in my own circle of friends.* ∎

**REFLECT**

What did Paul gain from taking Timothy with him—beyond companionship?

_____

_____

_____

**REFLECT**

Consider younger men in your life. Which ones could develop into a type of Paul/Timothy relationship in which you could pass on your spiritual insight?

_____

_____

_____

"**We can experience more of God's power when we allow others to believe in us.**"

# *A Spiritual Friendship*

Think of five people who have had a positive influence in your life. Try to think of people from your childhood as well as from adulthood. What were the traits these people had that made them such an influence in your life?

_____

_____

_____

_____

_____

**REFLECT**

Based on these traits, can you see yourself being more open with any of them? Which ones, and in what ways?

_____

_____

_____

**E**verything worthwhile in life is somewhat scary. Don't let fear block you from one of God's greatest blessings.

2 TIMOTHY 1:1–5
*Paul, an apostle of Jesus Christ by the will of God, according to the promise of life which is in Christ Jesus, to Timothy, my beloved son: Grace, mercy and peace from God the Father and Christ Jesus our Lord.*

*I thank God, whom I serve with a pure conscience, as my forefathers did, as without ceasing I remember you in my prayers night and day, greatly desiring to see you, being mindful of your tears, that I may be filled with joy, when I call to remembrance the genuine faith that is in you, which dwelt first in your grandmother Lois and your mother Eunice, and I am persuaded is in you also.*

The second letter to Timothy from Paul was written just prior to Paul's death. Though it is a somber letter, it begins warmly as Paul talked about their relationship. Over the years they had traveled together, had suffered and cried together, and had seen God work marvelous things through their ministry together. As old friends do, they had a lot of shared memories.

Timothy was a wealthy man when it came to friendship. In Paul, he had a friend who knew his weaknesses, yet still trusted him. When Timothy didn't do as well as Paul hoped he would in dealing with the Corinthian church, Paul was loyal to Timothy and remained committed to him. In reading Paul's letters to Timothy, we see that Paul was honest with Timothy, never pulling back from saying what needed to be said. Trust, loyalty, and honesty are each necessary traits for spiritual friendship.

Like Paul and Timothy, an older pastor and I had a spiritual friendship during my first church position in Florida.

He coached me and gave me the type of feedback that other people would never do. The first time I read the Scriptures aloud in church, this pastor pulled me aside for a little advice. "Go home and read it aloud five times before you read it in church." The advice felt intrusive but was extremely practical. Another time I spoke at a prayer meeting and he was in the audience. After I sat down, he handed me a brief note on a piece of paper.

"Have Jan sew up the pockets on your suit," it said. *Sew the pockets on my suit?* I scratched my head and wondered what it was about. While I spoke, I had a habit of sticking my hand in and out of my suit coat. He had noticed the distraction and suggested a solution. This modern day Paul-and-Timothy relationship made a lasting impact on my ministry.

Begin praying, if you haven't already, for God to direct you to that special friend who could also be a spiritual guide on your journey.

_____

_____

_____

Write down the names of those who come to mind, and then pray more specifically about how each one could assist in your spiritual growth.

_____

_____

_____

"Trust, loyalty, and honesty are each necessary traits for spiritual friendship."

*Lord, calm my fears and give me courage to pursue my spiritual friendships.* ■

# The One Jesus Loved

**Consider how your friends have demonstrated love toward you.**

_____

_____

_____

**List some practical ways that you have shown love to your friends.**

_____

_____

_____

**F**riends draw us into greater wholeness and genuine love and concern for others.

JOHN 21:20–22
_Then Peter, turning around, saw the disciple whom Jesus loved following, who also had leaned on His breast at the supper, and said, "Lord, who is the one who betrays You?"_

_Peter, seeing him, said to Jesus, "But Lord, what about this man?"_

_Jesus said to him, "If I will that he remain till I come, what is that to you? You follow Me."_

**I**f we think that Timothy had a unique friendship in Christian history because of his relationship with Paul, then the Apostle John had a friendship that is beyond comparison. We all know that Jesus loves us. "Jesus Loves Me" is the song that most of us learned in our early days of Sunday school. But it takes a special understanding of that love to be able to refer to yourself as the "disciple whom Jesus loved." Yet that's exactly the way John referred to himself.

Perhaps that's why John's Gospel is so different from the other three. John doesn't tell us anything about Jesus' birth. He doesn't quote a single parable. He gave us no temptation story or any instructions about communion. In _Peculiar Treasurers_, Beuchner said, "There's nothing he [Jesus] doesn't know in John, nothing he can't do, and when they take him in the end, you feel he could blow them right off the map if he felt like it. . . . Jesus, for John, is the Jesus he knew in his own heart and the one he believed everybody else could know too if they kept only their hearts open."

It takes a trusting relationship to keep your heart open. But John did just that and because he did, he knew the heart of God. Jesus knew John's heart as well. The way He loved him shaped John and everything he did, including the way John loved. That's why John could say so much about Jesus, the One who *is* love. In his Gospel and in his epistles, love is the central theme.

It's interesting to me that Jesus needed a best friend. He had the twelve disciples; out of that twelve, three were close friends, and one was His best friend. If manliness is defined as being strong enough that we don't really need anyone else, Jesus had it all wrong. But that's impossible. He's the one who made us.

It's just that narrow view of manliness that is all wrong—we need friends! We need friends in order to be strong, in order to grow, and in order to experience healing in our wounds. No one needs to regard himself as exempt from the need for friends—the Creator of the universe showed us in His life that He needed friends.

Friends can do something else for us as men. It's all too easy in our world today to have a singular focus, where all our energy is directed toward our career. Or we can become absorbed by our problems, looking inward and questioning everything. Friends draw us out into greater wholeness and concern for those around us. That's part of what Jesus meant when He said, "I am the vine and you are the branches." We need relationships.

*Lord, give me insight today how to reach out and love my friends.* ■

**REFLECT**

How have your friends helped you grow and heal your woundedness?

_____

_____

_____

**REFLECT**

How can you as a friend help your friends grow and move toward wholeness?

_____

_____

_____

"**We need friends in order to be strong, in order to grow, and in order to experience healing in our wounds.**"

# *Inner Authority*

**REFLECT**

What possesses you and arouses your passions?

_____

_____

_____

**REFLECT**

How do those things also control you in some way?

_____

_____

_____

JOHN 2:13–25

*Now the Passover of the Jews was at hand, and Jesus went up to Jerusalem. And He found in the temple those who sold oxen and sheep and doves, and the moneychangers doing business.*

*When He had made a whip of cords, He drove them all out of the temple, with the sheep and the oxen, and poured out the changers' money and overturned the tables. And He said to those who sold doves, "Take these things away! Do not make My Father's house a house of merchandise!"*

*Then His disciples remembered that it was written, "Zeal for Your house has eaten Me up."*

I've often imagined what it was like when Jesus cleared the moneychangers out of the temple area. It is interesting to me that no one stopped him or stood up to him and refused to move. Everyone left!

After the area emptied out, the religious leaders probably got together and appointed a committee. Maybe they called it a fact-finding task force. Following a hurried meeting where they took a first-hand look at the damage done by this stranger named Jesus, they set out to find him. When they found him, they approached him rather carefully.

How did they determine a spokesperson for their committee? Maybe he was chosen because he couldn't say no. He certainly does not seem to have been a forceful person. As I read the story, it seems like he apologetically approached Jesus and he asked, "Uh, sir, uh, could you perhaps, if you have the time, tell us by what authority you did what you did? That is, if it's not too much bother."

Obviously something about the presence of Jesus made other men hesitate. He had an internal sense

> **T**he old adage, "know thyself," is the key to finding inner authority as a man.

of authority that didn't need any external confirmation. If you were in His presence, then you felt His authority—whether you believed in Him or not.

It came from Jesus' self-possession. He was in complete control of who he was and how he acted around others. As God, He also "knew all men, and had no need that anyone should testify of man, for He knew what was in man" (John 2:24–25). That's godly manhood. We may not be able to know men in this way, but we can know what is within other men to some degree, and we can most certainly know ourselves better, becoming self-possessed as opposed to being possessed by other people or things.

One man, Peter, who I see in my counseling practice, is sort of a reactionary leader. Peter flares up and gets carried away with his point of view. Often he will be so forceful in explaining his position that others stop listening. But as we've worked on this area of Peter's life through the years, he has become someone who understands his limitations and is now able to express himself in a meeting or business situation with greater confidence and respect. Peter has changed from someone who is driven by status or prestige or income into someone who is driven by principles.

A wise old woman once told me: If you stand on the wrong principle of life, then you sacrifice the person. Make sure you don't take the wrong principle. The sense of self-possession comes from the inside and not some skill. Today, Peter understands himself and his importance, and he is more in tune with God's voice instead of his own.

*Lord, I want to look inside and see which principles guide my life. Please make those principles Your principles.* ∎

### REFLECT

How well do you know yourself?

_____

_____

_____

### REFLECT

Are you more naive than cynical? Or the other way around?

_____

_____

_____

> **"When we stand on principle, we need to make sure we aren't standing on the wrong principle."**

# A Man of Principle

**REFLECT**

Describe an experience where God was asking you to do something by faith that seemed to be at odds with your principles.

_____

_____

_____

**REFLECT**

How did you decide what to do?

_____

_____

_____

> **G**od is interested in more than "right-ness." He wants to move us to a deeper understanding of manhood.

MATTHEW 1:18–21

*Now the birth of Jesus Christ was as follows: After His mother Mary was betrothed to Joseph, before they came together, she was found with child of the Holy Spirit.*

*Then Joseph her husband, being a just man, and not wanting to make her a public example, was minded to put her away secretly. But while he thought about these things, behold, an angel of the Lord appeared to him in a dream, saying, "Joseph, son of David, do not be afraid to take to you Mary your wife, for that which is conceived in her is of the Holy Spirit. And she will bring forth a Son, and you shall call His name JESUS, for He will save His people from their sins."*

**O**n which principles do you base your daily decisions? Godly manhood is build on sound biblical principles. But sometimes God turns our principles upside down because He wants us to learn something even more important. For example, consider Joseph who did things by the book. He was a "just man," or in the New English Bible, he is described as "a man of principle" (Matt. 1:19 NEB).

His life was going along just fine. He was engaged to a beautiful young woman named Mary. They were following all the rules and customs for a young couple prior to marriage. Then, out of the blue, before Joseph had sexual intercourse with her, he found out she was pregnant.

It's easy for us to shrug and ignore this decision point for Joseph because we know the rest of the story. But when Joseph discovered this alarming fact, he didn't know anything else about the circumstances. In his quandary, Joseph wondered what to do. Mary told him a preposterous story about how her pregnancy was God's work and that no man had slept with her. But she *was* pregnant!

Joseph thought about his next step a long time.

Should he go ahead and marry her or should he break things off quietly and move on? In *Fathers and Sons* Gordon Dalby says, "A very genuine part of every man who reads this story wants terribly to say, 'Yes, Joseph, I'm with you. It's a tough choice, but leave Mary behind. Forget the woman you love. If a man doesn't have his principles, he's no man at all!'"

Fortunately, God stepped into the situation and resolved Joseph's predicament on principles. Through a visit from an angel, the Lord assured Joseph that Mary had told the truth. And Joseph moved from a man of principle to a man of faith. God honored his obedience.

A godly acquaintance of mine once alluded to a difficult situation in his marriage. Although he was a public figure, his wife was seldom seen in public. He could have chosen the easy way out—divorce. Instead, he chose to continue in his marriage and work toward a solution. Sometimes we look at what is easiest and act accordingly, but men like him remind us that first we need to ask God for His will and then follow in faith.

The two elements of faith and principle are not supposed to be in conflict, but sometimes God has a way of bringing them into collusion where we have to set aside the principles and simply believe God. That kind of decisiveness comes only as a part of the deeper qualities of masculinity.

*God, give me a deeper understanding of how to follow your principles in obedience.* ■

**REFLECT**

Describe an experience where God turned everything upside down as far as you expected.

_____

_____

_____

**REFLECT**

What lessons did you learn in those situations?

_____

_____

_____

"**God may turn our principles upside down because He wants us to learn something even more important.**"

# *The Confidence to Decide*

**REFLECT**

Describe some areas in your life where you have learned to trust God more quickly and can act more decisively.

_____

_____

_____

**REFLECT**

How did you learn those lessons about trusting God?

_____

_____

_____

**If only God would speak directly to me as He did those in the Bible, it would be so much easier to do what He wants me to do.**

MATTHEW 2:13–15

*Now when they had departed, behold, an angel of the Lord appeared to Joseph in a dream, saying, "Arise, take the young Child and His mother, flee to Egypt, and stay there until I bring you word; for Herod will seek the young Child to destroy Him."*

*When he arose, he took the young Child and His mother by night and departed for Egypt, and was there until the death of Herod, that it might be fulfilled which was spoken by the Lord through the prophet, saying, "Out of Egypt I called My Son."*

I have often said, "If only God would speak directly to me as He did those in the Bible, it would be so much easier to do what He wants me to do." Somehow, I have always felt that when God spoke to them, He spoke as a friend does to me—I literally see someone saying words to me that I hear and understand.

But the passage says that God spoke to Joseph through an angel in a dream. How did he know it was God and not something he ate? Obviously, Joseph had learned something about God's voice from his experience with God before his marriage. I don't think he sat around and debated very long about the message he heard, especially this time. It was a clear warning, and Joseph obeyed immediately.

He was a man who was self-possessed and who allowed himself to be God-possessed. When God spoke to him in this dream, Joseph acted decisively. Men who are comfortable with their true masculinity are decisive. They may delay action, weighing the options, but when the time comes to make the decision, they do it with confidence. They trust themselves to know not only themselves, but what God expects of them in a given situation.

Friends of ours have been pastoring the same church for twenty years. Now they are older and appear to be ready to retire. Instead, they have taken on a new challenge—they are moving to Japan as missionaries. They will be raising their own support as well as learning another language and culture. This decision for a couple in their sixties is surprising, but they didn't make a rash decision. This couple traveled to Japan and looked over the ministry situation firsthand; then they spent a long time praying and listening to God. Finally they made a decision in obedience and moved ahead. As they have gone to Japan, it hasn't been easy but they've not waffled in their obedience. They are self-possessed, able to weigh options and then move with decisiveness.

In our daily lives, each of us face decisions and new challenges in our job advancement, our families and our possessions. As we learn more about God and His Word, we increase our ability to weigh options and listen to God's voice and direction.

 **REFLECT**

Describe how you have discerned God's voice in your life in the past.

_____

_____

_____

 **REFLECT**

How does God speak to you now?

_____

_____

_____

> "**Knowing myself gives me the confidence to be decisive.**"

*Lord, thank You that You have spoken to me through Your Word. Help me to know it and then act on it.* ■

# *Stick Your Neck Out*

When you think of "sticking your neck out," what comes to mind?

_____

_____

_____

Will sticking your neck out make you a better man?

_____

_____

_____

> **W**hen our authority comes from within, we are able to stick our necks out with integrity.

MATTHEW 3:1–6

*In those days, John the Baptist came preaching in the wilderness of Judea, and saying, "Repent, for the kingdom of heaven is at hand!"*

*For this is he who was spoken of by the prophet Isaiah, saying: "The voice of one crying in the wilderness: 'Prepare the way of the LORD, make His paths straight.'"*

*And John himself was clothed in camel's hair, with a leather belt around his waist; and his food was locusts and wild honey.*

*Then Jerusalem, all Judea, and all the region around the Jordan went out to him and were baptized by him in the Jordan, confessing their sins.*

**J**ohn the Baptist fits the image of the wild man. Living alone in the desert, John the Baptist wore coarse clothes and ate strange food. When he talked with people, he approached them in a straightforward manner and wasn't afraid to speak the truth to anyone. He didn't take into consideration their rank or privilege when he spoke the truth.

The expectations of others didn't concern John the Baptist and he didn't care if he met those expectations. That's why he lived where he did, dressed as he did, and ate what he did. God's message was what mattered.

In *The Wild Man's Journey*, Richard Rohr and Richard Martos note that John the Baptist is much more like "God in the Old Testament (who) comes off much wilder than He does in the New Testament." God appears "in flaming bushes, in columns of smoke and fire, in clouds of thunder and lightning on mountain tops." To be wild is not the same as being crazy, although it may appear that way to some people. Rather, it is more a sense of being radical for the sake of the gospel. It involves sticking your neck out. In John the Baptist's case, he stuck his neck out too far and his head landed on Herod's platter.

In another sense, wildness means we stand firm with integrity because we are clear about who we believe in. According to many writers in the men's field, each of us has a wild man inside which we must come to terms with before becoming a man. The wild man loves to "rough it." Part of my wildness came out last year when I took a two-week train trip through Eastern Europe with my three grown sons. Ten years ago, I would never have ventured into that experience because I didn't know what I would talk about with my sons for two weeks. Back then, I would have been uptight about such a trip and depended on their mother to orchestrate the entire experience.

But last year my sons and I rode the train through Serbia. The conductor came through our car and showed us how to lower our blinds and lock our doors. We were entering a war zone. While it was a sobering time because of the danger, our socializing and fellowship as men was incredible. We enjoyed the opportunity to walk through the marketplace in Athens and stand and pray together on top of Mars Hill.

When we got home, we looked unshaven and a bit like wild men, but occasionally we need to reach inside and release the wild part of ourselves.

*Lord, give me the courage to face the wild part of myself.* ■

**What are some of the fears that hold you back?**

_____

_____

_____

**John the Baptist sacrificed his lifestyle for the sake of what and whom he believed in. In what ways do you sacrifice your lifestyle for what you believe in?**

_____

_____

_____

"**Each of us has a wild man inside that we must come to terms with before becoming a man.**"

# *The Wild Man of God*

**REFLECT**

In what ways do you struggle with your wild side?

_____

_____

_____

**REFLECT**

Is it an overpowering part of you, or a part you have repressed, or covered up in some way?

_____

_____

_____

**T**he man of God is a blend of John, the Beloved Disciple, and John the Baptist.

MATTHEW 11:1–6
*Now it came to pass, when Jesus finished commanding His twelve disciples, that He departed from there to teach and to preach in their cities. And when John heard in prison about the works of Christ, he sent two of his disciples and said to Him, "Are You the Coming One, or do we look for another?"*

*Jesus answered and said to them, "Go and tell John the things which you hear and see: The blind receive their sight and the lame walk; the lepers are cleansed and the deaf hear; the dead are raised up and the poor have the gospel preached to them. And blessed is he who is not offended because of Me."*

**T**o the very end, John the Baptist was not the sort of man that you would expect to have doubts. According to Patrick M. Arnold in *Wildmen, Warriors, and Kings*, John the Baptist was "unmanipulated, unbowed, unbeholden, undomesticated, unapologetic, and unashamed."

One of our common misconceptions is that the "wild man" never looks back. That's not the case at all. In this story, we see that later in his life, John the Baptist had doubts about the core issue of his work. Was Jesus really the Messiah? He was so concerned at one point that he sent a messenger to Jesus to ask the question directly. In typical fashion, Jesus gave an indirect answer, pointing instead to the fulfillment of Scripture in His ministry.

John the Baptist didn't fit our concept of a wild man. Each of us need to have a part that doesn't fit the mold. In my counseling practice, I see men in situations where things don't go the way that they think they should. These men are prepared to toss their faith in the air and jump off the horse. They say, "So much for this religious thing! God let me down." Their pain is so great, they stop their relationship with God.

I don't feel as though I'm any giant of the faith. Yet several years ago we went through a painful situation with one of our sons. As I look back on that painful time when I had many questions, I knew that I could question but I couldn't quit. Sometimes the pain hurt so much that I wanted to get off my horse of faith, but I couldn't let go of God's involvement.

John the Baptist questions but he never lets up. There is an honesty in that questioning. It involves a willingness for John to check it out himself and then hold on to what he knows is right.

None of us will probably go out into the desert and live in the wild like John the Baptist. But we need to know that wild part of ourselves and accept it as part of the underlying strength of our godly masculine nature. True manhood combines the gentleness of John, the beloved disciple, with the wildness of John the Baptist. Godly masculinity blends them both.

In a few words, describe your struggle.

_____

_____

_____

How do you work out the balance between the wildness of John the Baptist and the gentleness of John the Beloved?

_____

_____

_____

"**One of our common misconceptions is that the 'wild man' never looks back. That's not the case.**"

*God, I want to face honest questions yet preserve my faith in Your sovereignty. Amen.* ∎

# The New Taboo

**REFLECT**

Make an inventory of what you would have difficulty selling if Jesus said to you, "Sell all that you have."

_____

_____

_____

**REFLECT**

What would happen if you lost those things?

_____

_____

_____

LUKE 18:18–24

*Now a certain ruler asked Him, saying, "Good Teacher, what shall I do to inherit eternal life?"*

*So Jesus said to him, "Why do you call Me good? No one is good but One, that is, God. You know the commandments: 'Do not commit adultery,' 'Do not murder,' 'Do not steal,' 'Do not bear false witness,' 'Honor your father and your mother.'"*

*And he said, "All of these I have kept from my youth."*

*So when Jesus heard these things, he said to him, "You still lack one thing. Sell all that you have and distribute to the poor, and you will have treasure in heaven; and come, follow Me."*

*But when he heard this, he became very sorrowful, for he was very rich.*

*And when Jesus saw that he became very sorrowful, He said, "How hard it is for those who have riches to enter the kingdom of God!"*

I remember when sex was a forbidden subject. Next the subject of death and money became taboo. In *Freedom of Simplicity*, Richard Foster says that we have ways of showing our wealth, but we don't talk about it.

Perhaps you've been in a discussion with other men and the topic gets around to work and salaries. Regardless of how much we talk about our work, any discussion of salaries will become vague and guarded. Unless we're in a union or work where salaries are posted, we probably wonder if the guy next to us is making more than we are for doing the same thing.

Talking about how we spend our money is probably an even bigger taboo. When the pastor preaches on tithing, we are fine as long as he talks about the tithe, but he'd better stay away from

> **If we keep this area of our relationship with the Lord in the darkness or in the secrets of our heart, it will set us up for failure.**

discussing ideas like sacrifice or stewardship. We live in an area of Southern California where people have a lot of money.

Perhaps that's why it seems so intrusive to us for Jesus to tell this young man what he should do with his money. Why did Jesus ask for everything? The young man most certainly tithed, since he kept the law so meticulously. Many have interpreted this discussion as Jesus speaking out against riches or wealth. It seems more likely that He was pointing out to this young man, "This is what and who possesses you."

The rich young ruler was not self-possessed. That's why Jesus said to him: "You still lack one thing. Sell all that you have." There is a principle in this story about wealth. If we keep this area of our relationship with the Lord in the darkness or in the secrets of our heart, it will set us up for failure. Our wealth will end up owning us.

Some of our friends in Salt Lake City were very well off and generous with what they had. Through the years, they were faithful in their tithing and giving. Then their business took a sudden reversal and fell apart. These friends lost their business and home—yet they have no regrets. Now they work full-time in a ministry position. I've never seen anybody happier. They learned the wisdom of holding on to their possessions loosely.

*Lord, help me to hold my possessions loosely—and acknowledge them as a gift from your hand.* ■

### REFLECT

How would you handle that loss?

_____

_____

_____

### REFLECT

Have these things become a god to you?

_____

_____

_____

"**Wherever your treasure is, there will your heart be also.**"

# *Quiet Confidence*

**REFLECT**

What are some ways that you can listen to God?

_____

_____

_____

**REFLECT**

As we've looked this week at that inner confidence and authority found in different figures in the Bible, consider your life and describe some ways that you sense this inner authority at work.

_____

_____

_____

**T**he story of Samuel shows us that no situation is beyond God's touch. No wound or weakness is beyond his healing.

1 SAMUEL 3:8–10

*And the LORD called Samuel again the third time. Then he arose and went to Eli, and said, "Here I am, for you did call me." Then Eli perceived that the LORD had called the boy.*

*Therefore Eli said to Samuel, "Go, lie down; and it shall be, if He calls you, that you must say, 'Speak, LORD, for Your servant hears.'" So Samuel went and lay down in his place.*

*Then the LORD came and stood and called as at other times, "Samuel! Samuel!" And Samuel answered, "Speak, for Your servant hears."*

**I**n another chapter, we focused on Eli's sons and their poor relationship with their father. These sons were disobeying the laws of God and living like crooks. The work of God had moved far into the background of people's lives. Yet the evil practices of the priests continued and the people resented the fact that God did nothing to change things.

Apparently Eli told Samuel very little about God, even though Samuel had lived with his guardian Eli since childhood. Verse 7 says that "Samuel did not yet know the Lord, nor was the word of the Lord yet revealed to him." Eli had taught Samuel about the rituals of the priesthood, because that was how Eli supported the family. But Samuel had learned nothing about the God of Israel. What a sad commentary on the teaching of Eli.

The situation in Israel looked grim. Even the priesthood had lost their knowledge and zeal for God. Instead they continued in rituals of worship without knowing the Creator. Nevertheless, the story of Samuel shows us that no situation is beyond God's touch. No wound or lack is beyond His healing. Years before, Hannah had left her son Samuel with Eli, a priest. Then Eli raised Samuel, and this small boy was not unnoticed by God. The Lord had Samuel in the temple for a purpose. When it was time for that purpose to be fulfilled, God spoke directly to Samuel. In this case, Samuel heard a literal voice. In the middle of the night, the boy thought Eli was calling. Twice he stumbled out of bed and ran to Eli. Each time the priest told Samuel to go back to bed. Finally, after the third time, Eli realized that God was perhaps trying to say something to Samuel. The priest taught the boy how to respond, and Samuel did what he was told.

Through the experience, we see an inner strength in Samuel that made him become a great judge over Israel. He was not intimidated by Eli, or even by the voice of God. There was a quiet confidence in his response that said to the Lord, "Speak, for Your servant hears."

Each of us need this same sort of inner confidence in the God of the Universe. Then we also can turn and say, "Speak, Lord, for Your servant is listening."

In what situations do you still feel like a little boy inside, with very little authority or confidence?

_____

_____

_____

What do you think God wants to say to you in that area of your life?

_____

_____

_____

"**We need the quiet confidence of Samuel, so that we may say, 'Speak, for your servant hears.'**"

*Lord, give me ears to listen to You when You speak.* ■

# *The Grasshopper Complex*

**What are some of the things in your life that make you feel like a grasshopper?**

_____

_____

_____

**How do you respond to these things?**

_____

_____

_____

**NUMBERS 13:27–31**

*Then they told him [Moses], and said, "We went to the land where you sent us. It truly flows with milk and honey, and this is its fruit. Nevertheless the people who dwell in the land are strong; the cities are fortified and very large; moreover we saw the descendants of Anak there.*

*The Amalekites dwell in the land of the South; the Hittites, the Jebusites, and the Amorites dwell in the mountains; and the Canaanites dwell by the sea and along the banks of the Jordan."*

*Then Caleb quieted the people before Moses, and said, "Let us go up at once and take possession, for we are well able to overcome it."*

*But the men who had gone up with him said, "We are not able to go up against the people, for they are stronger than we."*

**C**ourage is another part of being a godly man. We're not necessarily referring to the type of courage we need when we voluntarily sky-dive out of an airplane for the first time, although that requires courage as well. This is a deeper trait, the kind of courage that Joshua and Caleb showed in today's passage. They returned from the land of Canaan after being sent there to spy out the land for Moses.

For forty days these men from each of the tribes of Israel toured Canaan, checking out the lay of the land, the fortification of the cities, and the military preparedness of the people. The spies brought back the fruit of the land and said, "It truly flows with milk and honey." The clusters of grapes were so large it took two men to carry them. Today the grape cluster is the symbol of tourism in Israel and refers back to these first tourists and one of their souvenirs.

> **"The grasshopper complex" doesn't take God's perspective into account.**

Ten of the twelve men gave the majority report, "We are like grasshoppers in our own sight." Their report about what they saw was probably accurate, but it led to great discouragement among the people. You can imagine the uproar that Caleb tried to quiet when it came his turn to give the minority report.

It takes a deep courage to be able to take an unpopular position, especially when the popular one is fueled by fear.

Several years ago a church board confronted their senior pastor about some inappropriate financial matters in the church. The pastor asked for more time to clarify the matter and in a matter of days had won over many of the board members to his viewpoint. Some of the board didn't believe the pastor and found some deeper courage for their position. In protest, they resigned. No additional steps of accountability were established for this senior pastor.

Five years after the incident, those board members who had the courage to resign saw the results of the inaction. This senior pastor was caught in a different issue regarding integrity. He left, but the incident was even more damaging to the church, and to its witness in the community. Fear had led some board members to compromise their earlier decision.

Fear has a way of maximizing the size of the obstacle and minimizing our own resources. Deep courage is not the bravery of the skydiver—it is based on a relationship with the God of the universe, the One for whom all things are possible.

*Lord, build some courage into my life—even if I have to take unpopular stances.* ∎

**REFLECT**

Where do you think Joshua and Caleb found the courage to stand alone against all of Israel?

_____

_____

_____

**REFLECT**

Where do you sometimes think you stand alone?

_____

_____

_____

> "It takes deep courage to be able to take an unpopular position."

# You and Your House

**REFLECT**

Write down some of the gods that clamor for your worship today. Consider simple ones like too much TV and subtle ones like greed.

_____

_____

_____

**REFLECT**

Think about the ones that you struggle with and write down a courageous action to change.

_____

_____

_____

**E**ach generation must make the choice to serve God. The courage of our choice gives courage to the next generation.

JOSHUA 24:14–18
*"Now therefore, fear the LORD, serve Him in sincerity and in truth, and put away the gods which your fathers served on the other side of the River and in Egypt. Serve the LORD! And if it seems evil to you to serve the LORD, choose for yourselves this day whom you will serve, whether the gods which your fathers served that were on the other side of the River, or the gods of the Amorites, in whose land you dwell. But as for me and my house, we will serve the LORD."*

*So the people answered and said: "Far be it from us that we should forsake the LORD to serve other gods; for the LORD our God is He who brought us and our fathers up out of the land of Egypt, from the house of bondage. . . . We also will serve the LORD, for He is our God."*

**J**oshua was a young man when he was sent to spy out the land of Canaan. Later, when it came time to enter and possess the Promised Land, Joshua was the general who planned the strategy for the whole process under the guidance of the Lord. He was certainly a courageous leader, and his courage was not superficial or some flash-in-the-pan type thing.

When we come to the end of his story, one wonders if he was still courageous as an old man. Yet we see an even deeper courage in him as he stood before the people in this instance. These people hadn't changed much from those days back in the wilderness. Now they had added local gods to their worship of Jehovah, and Joshua confronted them.

That took courage. It was just prior to the days when the Bible says that the people of Israel "did what was right in their own eyes" (see Judges 21:25). Obviously they had already started that process, for Joshua confronted them about making a choice: Serve the Lord or serve the gods of the Amorites. When they chose the Lord, Joshua told them to get rid of the foreign gods, and then he built a monument to mark their decision.

I wonder what the people of later generations thought as they passed by that monument on their way to worship the false gods and idols to whom they eventually returned. Had they been told anything about the choice their parents had made? Or perhaps had they even been among those who made that choice before Joshua?

Almost twenty years ago, few people were involved in home schooling. One of my friends was concerned about the fast-paced lifestyle in Southern California and wanted to get his family out of it. This couple put their concerns into action. They had a summer cabin at a Christian conference center in northern California. After winterizing the cabin in the fall, they moved their family in and schooled their two boys. When the winter snows fell, the family only got out about once a month. The family determined to take time and build some special truths from Scripture into the lives of their children. Recently we had dinner with one of the sons and he talked about the importance that year had in his development. Many people talk about making a commitment to their family—but this couple had the courage to act on their convictions.

Joshua's closing words, "As for me and my house, we will serve the Lord," stand as a testimony to courage. We need to have the courage to make that same choice each day.

*Lord, give me the courage to act on my convictions.* ■

**REFLECT**

Which have you successfully struggled against in the past? Describe your struggle.

_____

_____

_____

**REFLECT**

What markers or monuments have you built in your life to remind you that you and your house will courageously serve the Lord?

_____

_____

_____

**"As for me and my house, we will serve the Lord."**

# Courage in the Face of Fear

What do you do when your courage is confronted by very real and valid fears?

_____

_____

_____

REFLECT

What has been your experience with "fleeces"?

_____

_____

_____

> **B**e strong and of good courage . . . for the LORD your God, He is the One who goes with you (Deut. 31:6).

JUDGES 6:36–40

*Then Gideon said to God, "If You will save Israel by my hand as You have said—"look, I shall put a fleece of wool on the threshing floor; if there is dew on the fleece only, and it is dry on all the ground, then I shall know that You will save Israel by my hand, as You have said."*

*And it was so. When he rose early the next morning and squeezed the fleece together, he wrung the dew out of the fleece, a bowl full of water.*

*Then Gideon said to God, "Do not be angry with me, and let me speak just once more: Let me test, I pray, just once more with the fleece; let it now be dry only on the fleece, but on all the ground let there be dew."*

*And God did so that night. It was dry on the fleece only, but there was dew on all the ground.*

Is a courageous man ever afraid? It certainly appears to be that way. Look at Gideon. He laid out his fleece not just one night, but two. And each time God answered and told him that he was going to save Israel. With courage and confidence, Gideon then gathered together as many men as he could to prepare to do battle with the Midianites.

Just when everything was ready, God said to Gideon that he had too many men. Whatever fears Gideon had before, they were now multiplied as he watched over two-thirds of his army return home. But the 10,000 men left were still a good-sized army. But again God said, "Still too many!" And this time 9,700 men were sent home, leaving Gideon with only 300 men! A reasonable time for panic, it seems.

Did you ever notice God's gentle encouragement in this story? Just as the 300 men are about to start battle, God says, "But if you are afraid, go down to the camp with Purah your servant, and you shall hear what they say." Gideon did what God suggested and heard one of the enemy telling another of a dream he had just had predicting the defeat of the Midianites. When Gideon heard this, he worshipped God and won the battle.

Several years ago, my son was struggling with some addictive behavior. When he went through treatment, part of our involvement was to set some strong consequences for his behavior. As the leader of my family, I had been afraid to set limits. But in the context of a group and treatment, I was held accountable. It was scary to step out with that sort of courage. Only as I laid my situation before the Lord and through the encouragement of a group of people, we made it through the experience and our son changed his behavior.

Deep courage is the ability to stay with the task even when we are afraid. But it also includes the ability to be honest about our fears and to be able to lay them before the Lord. There is no hint of Gideon wavering in his calling. He just needed to face his fears and tap into God's reservoir of courage—something we need to do regularly as men.

How do you find courage and God's reassurance in situations where you are afraid?

_____

_____

_____

Have you ever had an experience like Gideon's where God seemed to strip away those things you were dependent upon? Describe it.

_____

_____

_____

> " Deep courage is the ability to stay with the task even when we are afraid. "

*God, help me to discover courage in the midst of my fears.* ■

# The Courage to Wait

**REFLECT**

**When have you found courage through waiting?**

_____

_____

_____

**REFLECT**

**Why is it sometimes difficult for you to wait?**

_____

_____

_____

> **T**wo of the foundations of courage are a sensitive heart and spiritual discipline.

NEHEMIAH 2:2–6

*Therefore the king said to me, "Why is your face sad, since you are not sick? This is nothing but sorrow of heart."*

*Then I became dreadfully afraid and said to the king, "May the king live forever! Why should my face not be sad, when the city, the place of my fathers' tombs, lies waste, and its gates are burned with fire?"*

*Then the king said to me, "What do you request?" So I prayed to the God of heaven.*

*And I said to the king, "If it pleases the king, and if your servant has found favor in your sight, I ask that you send me to Judah, to the city of my fathers' tombs, that I may rebuild it."*

*So the king said to me (the queen also sitting beside him), "How long will your journey be? And when will you return?" So it pleased the king to send me; and I set him a time.*

**S**ometimes we are intimidated by people who hold positions of power. But the deeper courage of godly masculinity is not intimidated by these people, even though it still honors that particular position. Nehemiah was a man whose courage came from the heart, and from the discipline of his spiritual life. When he heard about the plight of the Israelites in Jerusalem, he "sat down and wept, and mourned for many days" (Neh. 1:40). His heart was tender and sensitive. It also said that he "was fasting and praying before the God of heaven." That was his spiritual discipline.

Out of the grief over his kinsmen, and based on God's response to his fasting and praying, Nehemiah found the courage to speak directly to King Artaxerxes. Nehemiah had no status with the king, apart from his faithfulness and dependability. He was a servant who served wine to the king. He was not a government official. To do what he did could have not only ended his career as a wine server, it could have cost him his life. It took courage to act, and it took courage to believe that God was directing his steps.

We don't know how long Nehemiah waited before speaking to the king, but waiting is also a great act of courage. It is often much easier to be impulsive and jump right in. But godly courage seems to come to those who initially wait upon the Lord; there are times when waiting will give us the courage and wisdom we need.

One of my friends was a partner with several others in business. Several times Paul was given the opportunity to sell his portion of the venture but instead he waited. He didn't feel that the time was right to sell—despite the pressure from others. Recently Paul's circumstances changed and also the business shifted. Through these changes, his portion became much more valuable. Waiting dramatically increased the value and gave Paul the necessary wisdom to decide to sell.

Each of us face many decisions in our daily lives. Sometimes the most courageous step we can take is to wait before we take another step.

*Lord, give me the courage to know when to wait.* ∎

**REFLECT**

In relation to your spiritual discipline, which is more difficult for you—maintaining consistency or intensity? Describe it.

_____

_____

_____

**REFLECT**

Describe an experience where you found courage to deal with people in a position of authority.

_____

_____

_____

"**Godly courage comes to those who wait on the Lord.**"

# *The Foundation of Courage*

Describe a situation when you have experienced your courage supporting your natural abilities.

_____

_____

_____

When have you experienced your abilities being frustrated by your lack of courage?

_____

_____

_____

> **T**o complete a task takes more than talent; it takes courage as well.

NEHEMIAH 4:13–17

*Therefore I positioned men behind the lower parts of the wall, at the openings; and I set the people according to their families, with their swords, their spears, and their bows. And I looked and arose and said to the nobles, to the leaders, and to the rest of the people, "Do not be afraid of them. Remember the Lord, great and awesome, and fight for your brethren, your sons, your daughters, your wives, and your houses."*

*And it happened, when our enemies heard that it was known to us, and that God had brought their counsel to nothing, that all of us returned to the wall, everyone to his work.*

*So it was from that time on, that half of my servants worked at construction while the other half held the spears, the shields, the bows, and wore armor; and the leaders were behind all the house of Judah.*

**A**fter Nehemiah asked permission of the king to return to Jerusalem, he probably thought the worst was past. But when he arrived in Jerusalem, the former cupbearer learned that no one outside of Jerusalem really wanted the walls rebuilt.

Opposition started with ridicule, included slander and other acts of treachery, and continued through the threat of physical harm. This opposition must have made Nehemiah's already overwhelming task appear impossible.

But Nehemiah never missed a step. He handled each problem as it arose, and continued to encourage the people in their task. When the nobles and rulers tried to create confusion, Nehemiah talked with them face to face about the difficulties. With the priests and religious leaders, he held them accountable to their promises. At one point, Nehemiah even had to discern whether an informer was telling the truth or had been set up by his enemies. Nehemiah fought an all-out attack to discourage him from completing his task.

From the Scriptures, we can see the clear evidence of his daily walk and relationship with God. The courage for his situations didn't come from some character trait he inherited or from some personal charisma he possessed.

When Nehemiah began his task to rebuilt the wall, he didn't look back until the work was finished some fifty-two days later. If you read through the book of Nehemiah, you will marvel at his leadership abilities. The cupbearer knew how to divide people into manageable groups and then motivate them in monumental tasks. Even when the people were attacked, Nehemiah took it in stride and organized some people to guard the wall and others to continue building. While all of his organization and management skills are remarkable, his courage is at the foundation of that leadership. To complete a task takes more than talent, it takes courage as well.

 **REFLECT**

Describe what you think drained you of your courage.

_____

_____

_____

 **REFLECT**

What kinds of things are opposing you now in what you believe you need to do to be God's man?

_____

_____

_____

> **"The foundation of Nehemiah's courage was his openness to the Lord's direction in his life."**

*Lord, I need the courage to have you direct my life.* ∎

# Courage Grounded in Faith

**In which areas is God guiding your heart to do something different?**

_____

_____

_____

**Choose an area and make a plan about how the Lord wants you to make news.**

_____

_____

_____

> **Nothing restrains the Lord from saving by many or by few.**

1 SAMUEL 14:6–10
*Then Jonathan said to the young man who bore his armor, "Come, let us go over to the garrison of these uncircumcised; it may be that the LORD will work for us. For nothing restrains the LORD from saving by many or by few."*

*So his armorbearer said to him, "Do all that is in your heart. Go then; here I am with you, according to your heart."*

*Then Jonathan said, "Very well, let us cross over to these men, and we will show ourselves to them. If they say thus to us, 'Wait until we come to you,' then we will stand still in our place and not go up to them.*

*"But if they say thus, 'Come up to us,' then we will go up. For the LORD has delivered them into our hand, and this will be a sign to us."*

**S**aul's son Jonathan had a number of qualities that make him outstanding—integrity, loyalty, honor, truthfulness, and a number of other traits of godly masculinity. If God had not removed the kingdom from Saul, Jonathan would have made a great king. He certainly possessed great courage and faith. Only a man of faith would have said to his armorbearer that "nothing restrains the Lord from saving by many or by few." Just the two of them were taking on the Philistines. The story also shows that his armorbearer recognized the character of Jonathan because he quickly said that he would stand with Jonathan. He had no idea how many Philistines were there but was just anxious for some action and Jonathan trusted that God would direct him.

Was he simply a brash young man with no common sense? I don't think so. It appears that his father, the king, was being humiliated by the Philistines. Jonathan wanted to see what God would do if someone stepped out in faith and challenged their common enemy. And God acted on his behalf; Jonathan and his armorbearer killed about twenty men over about an acre of land. Then the Lord made an earthquake that created chaos in the camp of the Philistines—so much that they began killing each other. What had been a great humiliation became a great victory. It all happened because a young man had the courage to act on his faith in God. God was on Jonathan's side because Jonathan made sure he was on God's side. Instead of listening to the discouraging news at home, he went out and, with God's help, made news of his own.

Sometimes God stirs us to make a courageous act of faith. A couple of my missionary friends recently returned from the field because of health problems. They could have rested on their laurels and hit the speaking circuit. Instead, they returned home with a new vision—this couple wanted to create a place where missionaries could live, be refreshed, and even retire. They saw this venture as another opportunity to serve God in faith, so they stepped out. God has honored their courage and enabled them to begin a new ministry.

Maybe I'm facing a situation at work or home that is in a stall or a holding pattern. Instead of resting on my laurels, I can follow the example of Jonathan and ask the Lord for courage and faith to stretch into another opportunity. The unexpected is waiting around the corner.

*Lord, give me the courage to step out in faith.* ∎

**REFLECT**

Is there something that over the years you have felt God calling you to do or be that somehow has just never happened?

_____

_____

_____

**REFLECT**

In what ways might you still fulfill some of that earlier vision?

_____

_____

_____

"**Apart from the Lord, Jonathan's venture was a suicide mission.**"

# The Big Picture

**REFLECT**

When have you been too courageous, overstepping what you in-
tended or needed to do? Describe
what happened.

_____

_____

_____

**REFLECT**

In looking at your life, what percentage is lived circumstantially?

_____

_____

_____

**C**ourage comes from a
connection with the
heart of God, a connec-
tion that gives purpose
and direction beyond the
temporal things of life.

ACTS 16:27–33

_And the keeper of the prison, awaking from sleep and
seeing the prison doors open, supposing the prisoners
had fled, drew his sword and was about to kill himself._

_But Paul called with a loud voice, saying, "Do your-
self no harm, for we are all here."_

_Then he called for a light, ran in, and fell down
trembling before Paul and Silas. And he brought them
out and said, "Sirs, what must I do to be saved?"_

_So they said, "Believe on the Lord Jesus Christ, and
you will be saved, you and your household."_

_Then they spoke the word of the Lord to him and to
all who were in his house. And he took them the same
hour of the night and washed their stripes. And immediately he and all his family were baptized._

magine that you were thrown into jail for an
unjust reason. If an earthquake popped open
the doors, wouldn't you grab your coat and disappear? After all, you didn't deserve to be locked up in
the first place, why ask for trouble. No one could
fault you for slipping into the night.

But that approach is living life circumstantially,
and the Apostle Paul lived his life with a
larger purpose in mind. It takes godly
courage to be such a man. It also takes
courage to look at every situation—even
those that reek with injustice—and to understand that those situations are somehow fitting into God's purposes in our
lives.

Paul had that sort of deep courage. It
showed when he and Silas sang hymns at
midnight with chains on their feet and
open wounds on their backs. Then an
earthquake suddenly released their
chains and the prison doors flew opened. Paul's immediate concern was not for himself but for the
jailer. As I read through this story, I find it hard to

imagine how I would have thought to do the same thing.

The day after baptizing the jailer, the officials decided to release Paul and Silas from jail. But rather then slipping out of the city quietly, Paul and Silas knew they had been beaten and jailed unjustly. Instead they told the officials about their Roman citizenship. They asked that these magistrates escort them out of the city. Roman citizens? The magistrates knew that they were on thin ice. So with fear and trembling the officials came to the jail cell and begged Paul and Silas to leave the city. After attending to some business with Lydia, and also encouraging the brethren, they left for Thessalonica.

We can gain some good pointers about courage from the story of Paul and Silas. Courage comes from a connection with the heart of God, a connection that gives purpose and direction beyond the temporal things of life. It comes from my ability to see the big picture with God at the center, and then discern what the Lord wants me to learn, or to do, in an unexpected situation. Paul and Silas had the courage to listen as well as to act.

 **REFLECT**

What percentage of your life would you say is related to God's value system?

_____

_____

_____

 **REFLECT**

What changes are you going to make in your life to live more purposefully and to tap in deeper to God's enabling courage?

_____

_____

_____

" Knowing myself and why I behave as I do gives me more godly courage. "

*Show me the big picture for my life, Lord, and help me to keep it in focus.* ■

*Def. The reliability of ~~Gods Love~~*
↑ *Jesus "I am truth."*

# What Is Truth?

**How do you define truth?**

_____

_____

_____

**How do you know what is the truth in any given situation?**

_____

_____

_____

> **H**ow do we discover truth and know the Bible is true? We often wish we could have absolute proof that the Bible is true.

JOHN 18:33–38

*Then Pilate entered the Praetorium again, called Jesus, and said to Him, "Are You the King of the Jews?"*

*Jesus answered him, "Are you speaking for yourself on this, or did others tell you this about Me?"*

*Pilate answered, "Am I a Jew? Your own nation and the chief priests have delivered You to me. What have You done?"*

*Jesus answered, "My kingdom is not of this world. If My kingdom were of this world, My servants would fight, so that I should not be delivered to the Jews. . . ."*

*Pilate therefore said to Him, "Are You a king then?" Jesus answered, "You say rightly that I am a king. For this cause I was born, and for this cause I have come into the world, that I should bear witness to the truth. Everyone who is of the truth hears My voice."*

*Pilate said to Him, "What is truth?" And when he had said this, he went out again to the Jews, and said to them, "I find no fault in Him at all."*

**O**bviously, Pilate wasn't in the upper room with the disciples, so he hadn't heard Jesus say that He was the way, the truth, and the life. When Jesus told Pilate that his purpose was to bear witness to the truth, Pilate shrugged it off with a rather flip remark, "What is truth?" Apparently, Pilate was a modern man for his times. He would have fit right into today's culture.

Today we don't have much time for truth. We're too busy. Ultimate truth is for the academics to worry about. We've got business to conduct and people to hassle and households to provide for. And anyway, if we get too concerned with searching for truth, we usually stir up more trouble.

In Pilate's case, his close and unsatisfactory encounter with the truth stirred up something within him that he never got over. An old legend says that over and over again his body rises to the surface of a mountain lake in Switzerland and goes through the motions of washing its hands.

What Pilate missed was an opportunity not only to know the truth, but to have discovered a new reality. He missed it for a variety of reasons, but one of them was probably the idea that truth was some bit of data that you can identify.

Stretching the truth is an easy trap. A recent issue of *Success* magazine had an article on the art of deceitfulness as a management tool. According to the author, the most successful managers are those who know how to lie and lie well. How often do you hear, "The check is in the mail" or, "Yes, we can have it for you in a week," knowing full well that the deadline is impossible. Some days it is difficult to know who is telling the truth. Some of my clients struggle with little white lies. I've had them take a 3 x 5 card and write down every time they feel that they are stretching the truth.

How do we discover truth and know the Bible is true? We often think if only we could have absolute proof that the Bible is *true*. If only we could *prove* that Jesus rose from the grave. Then we would have the *truth*! We are making Pilate's mistake: We believe that a successful search for truth means to somehow come up with a list of proofs that support what we believe. This week, we will be looking at the Bible to answer the question: "What is

*Lord, I want to know the truth and to speak the truth day in and day out.* ∎

Describe an experience in which you thought you had the data to support the truth, and then found out you missed the point.

_____

_____

_____

Jesus says, "I *am* the truth." How does that affect your definition of *truth*?

_____

_____

_____

"Truth is more than knowledge; it encompasses our whole understanding of reality."

# The Spiritual Reality

**What could you do to think more about the spiritual reality around you?**

_____

_____

_____

**Often when we think of spiritual reality we think of Satan and his strongholds, but we overlook the reality of what Elisha and his servant saw—God's army of angels there to fight for us. Describe experiences where you have been very aware of God's spiritual forces at your side.**

_____

_____

_____

2 KINGS 6:13–17

*So the king of Syria said, "Go and see where Elisha is, that I may send and get him." . . . Therefore he sent horses and chariots and a great army there, and they came by night and surrounded the city. And when the servant of the man of God arose early and went out, there was an army, surrounding the city with horses and chariots. And his servant said to him, "Alas, my master! What shall we do?"*

*So he answered, "Do not fear, for those who are with us are more than those who are with them."*

*And Elisha prayed, and said, "LORD, I pray, open his eyes that he may see." Then the LORD opened the eyes of the young man, and he saw. And behold, the mountain was full of horses and chariots of fire all around Elisha.*

**T**his is one of those Bible stories where I would like to have stood by the shoulder of Elisha's servant. Then when Elisha prayed for the Lord to open the eyes of the servant, I would have liked to have seen the look on his face.

When the pair got up that morning and looked outside the city, it looked grim. The Syrian army had surrounded them and the servant knew that these soldiers were looking for his master, Elisha. The servant was terrified. You can catch the panic in his few words to Elisha.

Why wasn't Elisha afraid? Apparently the prophet had a different understanding of the truth. With human eyes, one could only see the Syrian army preparing to attack the city. But with God's eyes, the truth was completely different than what human eyes could see. When the servant's eyes were opened, he gained a deeper vision. The Syrian army was still in front of him, but

> **T**he physical reality is only a small part of God's reality. We need to broaden our vision to include the spiritual reality.

now he also saw that the mountains were full of horses and chariots of fire.

All too often, our search for truth is limited by our human perspective. All we can see is what is in front of us—only on the surface. When we speak of truthfulness as a part of our godly masculinity, we are speaking of a sense of knowing spiritual reality. Elisha was a man of God who could see what God saw. His young servant became more of a man when God opened his eyes to see the same things.

As we study the Scriptures and learn more about God's perspective and the spiritual dimension of our lives, then we begin to see a broader reality—a spiritual reality. When the situation around us looks desperate and there is no where to turn, we need to pray that God will open our eyes to see what He sees, including the spiritual realities around us.

*Open my eyes, Lord, to see the spiritual reality of my daily life.* ■

**REFLECT**

What situation are you struggling with now where you need to have your eyes opened to see God's hand at work?

_____

_____

_____

**REFLECT**

Describe your fears about this situation.

_____

_____

_____

"**Do not fear, for those who are with us are more than those who are with them.**"

# The Vapor of this Present Life

**REFLECT**

In what ways has your belief that things should be fair kept you from seeing God's ability to work in those situations?

_____

_____

_____

**REFLECT**

When we or someone close to us is the victim of someone else's power play, we often get angry. What have been the results if your anger has taken over in a situation like that?

_____

_____

_____

> **V**engeance isn't our concern; faithfulness is.

1 KINGS 21:13–16

*And two men, scoundrels, came in and sat before Naboth; and the scoundrels witnessed against him, against Naboth, in the presence of the people, saying, "Naboth has blasphemed God and the king!" Then they took him outside the city and stoned him with stones, so that he died.*

*Then they sent to Jezebel, saying, "Naboth has been stoned and is dead." And it came to pass, when Jezebel heard that Naboth had been stoned and was dead, that Jezebel said to Ahab, "Arise, take possession of the vineyard of Naboth, the Jezreelite, which he refused to give you for money; for Naboth is not alive, but dead."*

*So it was, when Ahab heard that Naboth was dead, that Ahab got up and went down to take possession of the vineyard of Naboth the Jezreelite.*

**T**his story about Ahab is the picture of a king who has no concept of spiritual reality, let alone the truth. He was a macho man, who was used to getting what he wanted because of his position and authority. And when he happened to meet someone who wasn't impressed by the fact that he was the king, his wife jumped in and created a solution. Standing for the truth will not always protect you. But living a lie will certainly lead to the removal of God's hand upon you.

In this story, King Ahab decided that he wanted to plant a vegetable garden near his palace in Samaria. As he looked around, Ahab noticed the vineyard of Naboth and decided that it was the perfect spot for a garden. When the king approached Naboth, at first he asked for Naboth to give him the property and then he offered to buy it. But Naboth was horrified at the thought of selling since the vineyard was part of his inheritance and may have been in his family for many years.

So Ahab sulked around the palace like a spoiled

little boy and his wife, Jezebel, schemed how to get the property that her husband wanted. In fact, Jezebel had two scoundrels falsely accuse Naboth of being a blasphemer against God. Based on the witness of two people, Naboth is taken outside the city and stoned. At first glance, we may think that society back then was unduly harsh. But in reality the story is little different from what happens today. People in many situations are still destroyed by untruths. They don't use just stones to finish off the evil business. Someone suddenly lost their job because they got caught in a power struggle and became expendable. They weren't stoned, but something died within them nonetheless. Perhaps you've seen that, or perhaps it's happened to you.

Being a godly man in that kind of situation means I look at the broader realities, especially the spiritual realities. I may not see God at work, but I know a broader picture from my past experiences, from the witness of Scripture, and from the experiences of my brothers in the Lord. I have learned that God never sleeps, never misses a thing, and is always deeply concerned with what is happening in my life.

But you may protest, "Naboth died." That's true. When we examine the spiritual realities, we are reminded that this present life is but a "vapor" (James 4:14). Beyond this life, there is so much more for us!

*Lord, help me to walk each day in faithfulness and leave the vengeance to your hand.* ■

**REFLECT**

Describe times when you have successfully kept God's perspective in a situation like Naboth's.

_____

_____

_____

**REFLECT**

What made the difference for you?

_____

_____

_____

> "When we examine the spiritual realities, we are reminded that this present life is but a vapor."

# Don't Help God Out

When have you tried to help God out in some situation in your life or the life of your family?

_____

_____

_____

In what ways was your vision limited to the present reality?

_____

_____

_____

**GENESIS 27:15–20**

*Then Rebekah took the choice clothes of her elder son Esau, which were with her in the house, and put them on Jacob her younger son. And she put the skins of the kids of the goats on his hands and on the smooth part of his neck. Then she gave the savory food and the bread, which she had prepared, into the hand of her son Jacob.*

*So he went to his father and said, "My father"; and he said, "Here I am. Who are you, my son?"*

*And Jacob said to his father, "I am Esau your firstborn; I have done just as you told me; please arise, sit and eat of my game, that your soul may bless me."*

*But Isaac said to his son, "How is it that you have found it so quickly, my son?" And he said, "Because the LORD your God brought it to me."*

**E**ver feel like you needed to "help God out"? I have. I remember setting up situations within my family for the sake of one person, hoping that God would work His miracle. And He didn't—at least not the way I expected.

A couple that I know entered their daughter in a counseling program and were full of confidence that this program would be just the breakthrough that their daughter needed. The daughter got into the program, and her father Kirk called in different favors that his friends owed him. He wanted to do anything to get his daughter back on track. She did enter the program, but the counseling didn't result in any consistent changes. Before long, she fell back into her old patterns. The answer for Kirk's desire for a change in his daughter happened months later—in a completely unexpected and unpredictable manner. So often it is God's timing for a situation and not ours.

In the Bible story for today, Rebekah set things up with Jacob so that he could get the blessing from

> **W**e need to remember that if God's timing seems to be a problem, God can even handle that.

Isaac—and insure God's promise that the younger son would rule over the older son (see Gen. 5:23). Whenever I read this story, I wonder what God would have done if Rebekah hadn't have been so manipulative, or if Jacob had had more backbone and had stood up to his mother's deceit. How would God have worked out the promise He had made to Rebekah before the birth of her sons?

We'll never know. But I am certain that God had His own plan about how that would occur. God doesn't really need us to meddle in His divine plans, either for ourselves or those we love. Of course, I think the Lord would love for us to participate in His plans, but not for us to take charge.

We are most often tempted to step in when our vision is limited to temporal reality. If that is the only reality we know or acknowledge, then it is easy to see why Rebekah panicked and set up this charade! But when we know about a reality that transcends this world and this life, we can depend on God to follow through on His promises—regardless of how hopeless or complicated this present reality appears to us.

 **REFLECT**

What were the results of your limited vision?

_____

_____

_____

 **REFLECT**

When we looked at courage, we looked at the importance of waiting. In what ways does your limited vision of reality make it difficult to wait for God's timing in a situation?

_____

_____

_____

> **"God doesn't need us to meddle in divine plans, either for ourselves or for those we love."**

*God, give me the patience to trust You for my every concern.* ∎

# *The Truth about Ourselves*

**REFLECT**

When have you been confronted by someone who opened your eyes to your own failure or sin?

_____

_____

_____

**REFLECT**

How did you respond to the truth in that situation?

_____

_____

_____

**A**nd you shall know the truth, and the truth shall make you free (John 8:32).

2 SAMUEL 12:1–5, 7

*Then the LORD sent Nathan to David. And he came to him, and said to him: "There were two men in one city, one rich and the other poor. The rich man had exceedingly many flocks and herds. But the poor man had nothing, except one little ewe lamb which he had bought and nourished; and it grew up together with him and with his children. It ate of his own food and drank from his own cup and lay in his bosom; and it was like a daughter to him.*

*"And a traveler came to the rich man, who refused to take from his own flock and from his own herd to prepare one for the wayfaring man who had come to him; but he took the poor man's lamb and prepared it for the man who had come to him."*

*Then David's anger was greatly aroused against the man, and he said to Nathan, "As the LORD lives, the man who has done this shall surely die! . . ."*

*Then Nathan said to David, "You are the man!"*

**O**ne evidence that godly masculinity is growing within us includes our increasing ability and desire to know the truth about ourselves. It is more than a realization that we are sinners—in particular, it is the realization of how we are sinners.

David had a sensitive spirit. He had to know that it was wrong for him to have lusted after Bathsheba. His conscience had to be bothering him when he arranged for Uriah's death in the battle. How could David live with himself after these horrendous acts?

Each of us are made with a denial system that can block out the reality of our behavior. Apparently, David successfully blocked out of his mind what he had done, and carried on with his life.

When we do this, God has means of restoring our vision. Nathan the prophet told a story that made David angry at the unjust behavior of a man who had everything. Since Nathan had David's attention, he said to him, "You are the man!" and David's eyes were opened.

I believe that God loved this aspect of David's character. He could see the truth when it was presented to him. There was no blaming, no rationalizing, no excuses. David simply acknowledged— "I have sinned against the Lord." Yes, he had sinned against Bathsheba and Uriah, but also his greatest sin was against the Lord, and he acknowledged it.

The Scriptures tell us that David was a man after God's own heart. Even though he sinned, he remained close to God because he acknowledged his sin, asked for forgiveness, and then walked in righteousness.

**How do you wish you had responded to the truth in that situation?**

_____

_____

_____

**Who is in your life to tell you the truth even if it hurts?**

_____

_____

_____

> **"David saw the truth when it was presented to him. There was no blaming, no rationalizing, no excuses."**

*Lord, give me courage to face the truth and honestly deal with it.* ∎

# Honest Doubt

## REFLECT

Be honest and open as you consider: What are some of the things you have doubts about in your relationship with God?

_____

_____

_____

## REFLECT

What has made it difficult in the past to openly express some of the questions you had about your faith?

_____

_____

_____

**Truthfulness includes being honest about what we feel, including our doubts.**

JOHN 20:24–29

*But Thomas, called Didymus, one of the twelve, was not with them when Jesus came. The other disciples therefore said to him, "We have seen the Lord." But he said to them, "Unless I see in His hands the print of the nails, and put my hand into His side, I will not believe."*

*And after eight days His disciples were again inside, and Thomas with them. Jesus came, the doors being shut, and stood in the midst, and said, "Peace to you!"*

*Then He said to Thomas, "Reach your finger here, and look at My hands; and reach your hand here, and put it into My side. Do not be unbelieving, but believing."*

*And Thomas answered and said to Him, "My Lord and my God!"*

*Jesus said to him, "Thomas, because you have seen Me, you have believed. Blessed are those who have not seen and yet have believed."*

Do you ever have any doubts? Another part of truthfulness is to be able to honestly face your feelings—even your doubts. Many of us were taught that it is wrong to doubt—we must always have faith. We have heard sermons on Thomas the doubter, and somehow got the idea that Thomas was less of a disciple because he questioned what the others said about seeing Jesus. Thomas wasn't present the first time that Jesus appeared to His disciples. Although Jesus had predicted His death and resurrection, the idea of someone coming back from the grave was a new one.

Before he believed, Thomas wanted some actual proof. He told the other disciples, "Unless I see in His hands the print of the nails, and put my finger into the print of the nails, and put my hand into His side, I will not believe." That's honesty!

Jesus never rebuked Thomas for his doubt. In fact,

when the Lord finally appeared in the presence of Thomas, Jesus responded very specifically to Thomas's request. Jesus' statement about blessed are those who believe without seeing was not a rebuke for Thomas, but a blessing to those who believe simply on the basis of their faith.

I'm not sure why we don't talk with God about our doubts. Maybe we want to shield God from our disbelief, or possibly we want to protect ourselves from the judgment of others who don't identify with our struggles. Both are unnecessary. We certainly don't need to protect God from any of our emotions. Doubt, anger, frustration—none of these intimidate God. Our honest doubts do not threaten God's self-perception anymore than the self-perception of Jesus was threatened by Thomas's honest questions. God always appreciates honesty.

And if we properly understand grace, we need not fear the judgment of our fellow believers. If each of us were honest, we would acknowledge that we go through periods when it is difficult to trust a God that we cannot see. And we can be sure that God cares about our honest concerns and will meet us at the point of our struggle.

**REFLECT**

How did you deal with those difficulties?

_____

_____

_____

**REFLECT**

What do you honestly need from God today that is similar in some ways to what Thomas needed from Jesus?

_____

_____

_____

> **"Jesus never rebuked Thomas for his doubt."**

*Lord, I want to face the truth with honesty—including my doubts.* ∎

# *To Know the Truth*

## REFLECT

What area of your life needs to be opened more to God's way of seeing things?

_____

_____

_____

## REFLECT

What are some of your fears about letting go of your limited vision and seeing more of the spiritual reality?

_____

_____

_____

JOB 27:2–6
*"As God lives, who has taken away my justice,*
*And the Almighty, who has made my soul bitter,*
*As long as my breath is in me,*
*And the breath of God is in my nostrils,*
*My lips will not speak wickedness,*
*Nor my tongue utter deceit.*
*Far be it from me*
*That I should say you are right;*
*Till I die I will not put away my integrity from me.*
*My righteousness I hold fast, and will not let it go;*
*My heart shall not reproach me as long as I live."*

**T**he theology of Job's day said that God blessed the righteous and punished the sinner.

**J**ob was surrounded by people who were urging him to simply say or do whatever it took to stop the torture. When God gave Satan permission to play havoc with Job's life, his world suddenly crumbled. His children were killed, his crops destroyed, and his animals kidnapped. Then Satan attacked Job's body, and he broke out in boils from his head to the soles of his feet.

His wife suggested that he curse God and die. His friends argued endlessly that Job must have done something wrong, because the theology of his day said that God blessed the righteous and punished the sinner. Since Job's world was falling apart and he was being punished, obviously Job had sinned, and he simply needed to admit it then get on with his life.

One good aspect of the comments of Job's so-called comforters was to mobilize Job's anger in his own defense. Without these "friends" who prodded Job into defense, he probably would have turned his anger inward upon himself and his helplessness to understand his situation. But Job's friends persisted in telling him about his faults in life. It allowed Job to see his problem with greater clarity; something else was going on.

The truth was important to Job. He wanted to get to the bottom of things, no matter what it cost him. Since he had lost almost everything already, Job figured that little else mattered. He held on to his own integrity and demanded the truth. Job wasn't concerned about knowing the truth so it would benefit him in any way; he wanted to know truth for the sake of knowing what is objectively true and fair.

At the end of the book, when he finally repented, Job held on to his righteousness in terms of his behavior. He repented of his limited view of spiritual reality and of God. Job realized that he could not understand the purposes of God—even when God addressed him directly. In the final chapter, Job said, "I have heard of You by the hearing of the ear, but now my eye sees You. Therefore I abhor myself, and repent in dust and ashes" (Job 42:5–6).

God challenged Job to grow in his weak point. His vision needed to be expanded to see his life more as God saw it. As we face a world of suffering and trials, we need to follow Job's example and turn to God. Ask the Lord of the Universe to give you spiritual eyes to see your situation for a broader purpose than the pieces of the puzzle that are before you.

**When have you been in a bind and tried to help God out?**

_____

_____

_____

**Write out your commitment to allow God to expand your vision so that you will see more of the spiritual realities around you.**

_____

_____

_____

> "**Godly manhood is always infused with integrity.**"

*Lord, no matter what happens to my life, permit me to walk with You in integrity.* ∎

# Responsibility Is Action

**REFLECT**

Describe a time when you acted responsibly.

_____

_____

_____

**REFLECT**

Describe a time when your passivity in a situation became irresponsibility.

_____

_____

_____

> **R**esponsibility is not passivity. It is action taken in accordance with God's plans.

JOSHUA 7:10–12, 15

*So the LORD said to Joshua: "Get up! Why do you lie thus on your face? Israel has sinned, and they have also transgressed My covenant which I commanded them. For they have even taken some of the accursed things, and have both stolen and deceived; and they have also put it among their own stuff.*

*"Therefore the children of Israel could not stand before their enemies, because they have become doomed to destruction. Neither will I be with you anymore, unless you destroy the accursed from among you. . . .*

*"Then it shall be that he who is taken with the accursed thing shall be burned with fire, he and all that he has, because he has transgressed the covenant of the LORD, and because he has done a disgraceful thing in Israel.'"*

**O**ften with our children, we use the word *responsibility*. We wish they would learn this important trait early. Its definition is quite accurate for parents teaching their children—the desire that they would do what they need to do without our forcing them to. We want them to initiate action, and that is the characteristics of godly masculinity. Responsibility is the opposite of passivity.

Joshua typifies responsibility. As the Israelites moved into the Promised Land, Joshua took charge. He led the people as he walked in step with God and worked out God's plan for their actions. But when the people prepared to attack a small city called Ai, Joshua believed only a few of the men needed to go into battle. The battle didn't go according to Joshua's plans.

The Israelites fled from before the men of Ai, not because they were outnumbered, but because the hearts of the people melted and became like water. There was sin in the camp and God was not with them during their battle.

But Joshua didn't know the reasons behind the defeat. In despair, he flung himself before God and pleaded his case in terms of the larger picture. I love it the way God said to him, "Get up! Why do you lie thus on your face?"

Did you ever have God say to you, "Stop praying and get busy. We've got a problem to solve!" That's exactly what he told Joshua. There was sin in the Israelite camp, and it had to be rooted out before they could go on.

Apparently there is a time to pray and there is a time to take action. As a responsible man, Joshua was sensitive to which action God wanted him to take. He got up and found out that Achan had disobeyed God by taking some of the treasure of Jericho. That irresponsible action from Achan had cost the lives of thirty-six men when they attacked the city of Ai. The godly man is willing to take responsibility even for the problems he encounters and to work to repair the problems.

**REFLECT**

**What were the consequences of your irresponsible actions?**

_____

_____

_____

**REFLECT**

**On a scale of 1 to 10, with 1 being poor and 10 being fantastic, how good are you are sizing up a situation, seeing what needs to be done, and then either doing it or seeing that it gets done?**

1  2  3  4  5  6  7  8  9  10

"**Did you ever have God say to you, 'Stop praying and get busy. We've got a problem to solve'?**"

*God, I need Your help to act responsibly with my daily decisions.* ■

# *Own Up to It*

**REFLECT**

How difficult is it for you to take responsibility for your behavior and actions when you have done the irresponsible thing?

_____

_____

_____

**REFLECT**

In what ways have you improved in the area of responsibility?

_____

_____

_____

**It's the age old conflict between responsibility and irresponsibility.**

EXODUS 32:19–20, 22–24

*So it was, as soon as he came near the camp, that he saw the calf and the dancing. So Moses' anger became hot, and he cast the tablets out of his hands and broke them at the foot of the mountain. Then he took the calf which they had made, burned it in the fire, and ground it to powder; and he scattered it on the water and made the children of Israel drink it. . . .*

*So Aaron said, "Do not let the anger of my lord become hot. You know the people, that they are set on evil. For they said to me, 'Make us gods that shall go before us; as for this Moses, the man who brought us out of the land of Egypt, we do not know what has become of him.'*

*"And I said to them, 'Whoever has any gold, let them break it off.' So they gave it to me, and I cast it into the fire, and this calf came out."*

Aaron was the number two man in Israel. Moses was the leader and Aaron the second in command. When Moses saw the burning bush in the Midian desert, God asked him to return to Egypt and free the people. Moses said he wasn't a good enough speaker so he asked if Aaron could speak for him. God agreed with the choice and must have felt that Aaron had some leadership abilities, including the ability to act responsibly.

When Moses went up on the mountain to receive the laws of God, he was away for a long time. The people grew restless and began to think that Moses had forsaken them. They decided that they wanted Aaron to be their leader. They wanted an image that they could see and worship, so Aaron took charge.

If responsibility means only the ability to take action, Aaron was acting responsibly. But it is more than that. It is action in accord with God's plans. And Aaron forgot completely about God. So when the people came and asked him to make "us gods that shall go before us," Aaron, who knew better, did as the people requested.

One interesting point in this passage is Aaron's explanation for what happened. He did not accept the responsibility for his actions against God. Instead, he told Moses an exaggeration. Aaron said the people gave him gold, "and I cast it into the fire, and this calf came out." Which is another way of saying, "I don't know how it happened, Moses. I just put the gold in the fire and *bingo*, all of a sudden there was this calf. Beats me how it happened."

Does that sound like something we have said in similar circumstances? There are always those who will act in accordance and obedience to God's plans. But there are others who ignore God's plans and somehow rationalize their actions. It's the age-old conflict between responsibility and irresponsibility. The godly man assumes responsibility.

 **REFLECT**

What kinds of responsibility and irresponsibility did you see in your father when you were growing up? How has that affected you?

_____

_____

_____

**REFLECT**

Is there some situation where you acted irresponsibly that you need to correct? Describe it and what you will do to correct it.

_____

_____

_____

> "It's better to own the responsibility than to try to regain it after it has been lost."

*Lord, help me to have the courage to act responsibly and in accordance to Your will.* ∎

# *R*esponsibility for Others

**REFLECT**

**What have you given up so that someone new to the faith or weaker in faith wouldn't stumble?**

_____

_____

_____

**REFLECT**

**How did you decide the situations described above?**

_____

_____

_____

> **I**f our freedom causes a brother who is weaker in the faith to stumble, then we haven't just wounded him, we have sinned against Christ.

1 CORINTHIANS 8:8–13

*But food does not commend us to God; for neither if we eat are we the better, nor if we do not eat are we the worse. But beware lest somehow this liberty of yours become a stumbling block to those who are weak.*

*For if anyone sees you who have knowledge eating in an idol's temple, will not the conscience of him who is weak be emboldened to eat those things offered to idols? And because of your knowledge shall the weak brother perish, for whom Christ died?*

*But when you thus sin against the brethren, and wound their weak conscience, you sin against Christ. Therefore, if food makes my brother stumble, I will never again eat meat, lest I make my brother stumble.*

**S**ometimes in exercising responsibility, we will be forced to reject a course of action that may well be a perfectly good thing to do. As responsible men, we need to be able to read the situation.

Paul described such a situation. Apparently, if you went to the meat market in Corinth, the best cuts of meat came from animals that had been offered to idols. The other meat was of lower quality. So why not eat the good meat? Paul found no difficulty in terms of his own conscience in eating meat that had been offered to idols. The Corinthian church was struggling with this issue. What's an idol anyway except for a piece of wood or stone? It has no life or power. What difference does it make to the meat if it has been offered to an idol?

Now Paul's attitude wasn't shared by everyone. In Corinth there were new believers that had been converted from religions that worshipped idols. To eat the meat offered to idols felt to them as though they were still in the old bondage. They couldn't enjoy the freedom Paul felt. For Paul, then, the question became, "Can I still eat this meat if it offends my brother? What is the responsible thing to do?"

Paul's answer was clear. If our freedom causes a brother who is either weaker in the faith or new to the faith to stumble, then we haven't just wounded him, we have sinned against Christ. Paul was so concerned about acting responsibly that he went so far as to say he would never eat meat again if that's what it took to keep a brother from stumbling.

Love was the critical ingredient that drove Paul to his conclusion. As he wrote earlier in the same chapter, "Knowledge puffs up, but love edifies. And if anyone thinks that he knows anything, he knows nothing yet as he ought to know. But if anyone loves God, this one is known by Him" (1 Cor. 8:1–3).

As believers, we have freedom in Christ. But as we love our brothers and sisters, we don't want to act irresponsibly toward them. Today our culture doesn't struggle with meat offered to idols. But there are on-going discussions about other issues which cause people to stumble like the use of alcoholic beverages. One person will find the freedom to have a glass of white wine with supper but another who has come from an alcoholic background will find it entirely offensive. We need to celebrate our freedom in Christ but also act responsibly to others around us.

*Lord, give me the sensitivity to act responsibly toward my brothers and sisters in Christ.* ∎

**REFLECT**

There is often an inner conflict between not causing a brother to stumble and being true to yourself and your convictions. In Paul's mind, there is no conflict—he will sacrifice his own desires for the sake of his brother. How have you handled that conflict?

_____

_____

_____

**REFLECT**

Describe ways you can be sensitive to those around you in the faith.

_____

_____

_____

**"Our freedom in Christ is always tied to our responsibility to our brothers and sisters."**

# Truth and Consequences

**REFLECT**

Describe some situations where you knowingly or unknowingly tried to shift the blame away from yourself. What were you trying to protect in yourself?

_____

_____

_____

**REFLECT**

How did others close to you respond when you shifted the blame from yourself?

_____

_____

_____

GENESIS 3:9–13

*Then the LORD God called to Adam and said to him, "Where are you?"*

*So he said, "I heard Your voice in the garden, and I was afraid because I was naked; and I hid myself."*

*And He said, "Who told you that you were naked? Have you eaten from the tree of which I commanded you that you should not eat?"*

*Then the man said, "The woman whom You gave to be with me, she gave me of the tree, and I ate."*

*And the LORD God said to the woman, "What is this you have done?" And the woman said, "The serpent deceived me, and I ate."*

There is a binding relationship between an act and its consequences that we cannot escape. Even Adam and Eve tried to blame someone else for their own conduct. Adam blamed his wife, Eve blamed the serpent. Although they tried to pass off their actions on someone else, they couldn't ignore the connection between the acts and their consequences. They are inseparable.

If that is a truth that we understand, why is it that we so often act just like Adam? We blame the person closest to us for our action, hoping to escape the consequences. In our blaming, we act irresponsibly, and that keeps us stuck in a shallow form of masculinity. We know little of what it means to be "God's man."

A. W. Tozer wrote in *Of God and Man* about the need for "better Christians." He recognized that idea as somewhat foreign to us, for we often see ourselves as alike, as equal because we are all God's forgiven children. But he points out that "a Christian is a born-one, an embodiment of growing life, and as such may be retarded, stunted, undernourished, or injured very much as any other organism."

> **G**rowth can only take place when we responsibly take ownership of our condition and seek to change it.

Growth can only take place when we responsibly take ownership of our condition and seek to change it. Tozer noted the story of a church father, Macarius of Optino, who when complimented for some help he gave, replied, "This cannot be. Only the mistakes are mine." We may think of that as a bad self-image in today's way of thinking, but his words reflect a sense of responsibility that we often lack.

Years ago, I was on the church staff in Pasadena. When I was driving home one day, a car crept ahead of me in traffic and I hit it. The driver was very upset with me and told me to pull over, but I kept on driving. So the man flagged down a policeman and chased me. Technically, I had committed a hit and run accident. Although I wasn't arrested, I was caught and the little damage to the other car cost me about $100. For the policeman, he considered it a minor incident but for me, it made a major impression of my own failure to act responsibly. In my church responsibilities, I was teaching an adult Sunday school class and felt compelled to share the incident with my class. They needed to know my own failures and my own intention to keep on growing as a believer.

We love to take the glory and the credit, but we will do anything to avoid taking the responsibility and blame. Godly manhood is a result of spiritual growth, and that growth is fed by our ability to take responsibility for our actions.

**REFLECT**

Is there a situation you are currently involved in where you are being blamed in some way, and you are trying to shift the blame to where you think it belongs? It's often easier to see the speck in someone else's eye than to see the stick in our own. To what degree might that be true in this situation?

_____

_____

_____

**REFLECT**

Describe a situation in which you have avoided taking responsibility for the consequences. Write out your commitment to be a responsible man in that situation.

_____

_____

_____

*God, I want to accept the responsibility for my actions and seek to change them.* ■

**"There is a genuine humility in the man who can take responsibility for his actions."**

# Taking the Initiative

**REFLECT**

Are you waiting for someone else to take responsibility in some area of your life? Describe the situation.

_____

_____

_____

**REFLECT**

As you wait, what makes you think someone else will be responsible?

_____

_____

_____

MATTHEW 18:10–14

*"Take heed that you do not despise one of these little ones, for I say to you that in heaven their angels always see the face of My father who is in heaven. For the Son of Man has come to save that which was lost.*

*"What do you think? If a man has a hundred sheep, and one of them goes astray, does he not leave the ninety-nine and go to the mountains to seek the one that is straying?*

*"And if he should find it, assuredly, I say to you, he rejoices more over that sheep than over the ninety-nine that did not go astray. Even so it is not the will of your Father who is in heaven that one of these little ones should perish."*

**T**his is a well-known parable that has been the subject of songs and paintings over the centuries. In many ways, it speaks of the love of God for each of us, and of the searching heart of the God who seeks those who are lost. We have all been the lost sheep that God so faithfully searched for and found.

There was also an important principle illustrated in this parable that I haven't heard mentioned very often. To illustrate that trait, it might help to think back to a situation that we have in common. Was there ever a time when you and someone else were in separate vehicles trying to get to the same place? Somehow you get separated, and you arrive at the destination. After waiting for some time for your friend to arrive, someone says, "Oh, I bet he's lost." And then someone else says, "Yeah, but he'll figure it out and find us."

Several years ago I was driving around with our family in France. We were supposed to stay with some missionary friends and I had gotten directions and thought I had followed them exactly. But I

> **"Oh, they'll figure out a way" is not part of the lexicon of a responsible shepherd.**

didn't reach their house. I was hopelessly lost on the streets but determined not to have to call them again. I returned to my starting point and tried again, and again, and again. No way was I going to call these friends and admit my error. Finally we reached the destination and our friends were worried that something had happened. I hadn't taken the initiative and called back for better directions.

In the parable of the lost sheep, Jesus makes it clear that the Shepherd doesn't act that way. Instead, God takes the initiative. He takes responsibility, even though He is not the one who is lost. He chooses responsibly to go and find the one who is lost. "Oh, they'll figure out a way" is not part of the lexicon of a responsible shepherd.

That's an important part of the trait of responsibility—When we act responsibly, we don't wait for someone else to do what needs to be done, we do it. The principle is always the same: The one who is more mature, more capable—that's the one who takes the initiative and the responsibility.

 REFLECT

Describe some of the fears you may have that cause you to wait for someone else to take over.

_____

_____

_____

 REFLECT

Is there a situation within your family where you need to act more responsibly? List the steps you will take to correct that situation.

_____

_____

_____

> "When we act responsibly, we don't wait for someone else to do what needs to be done; we do it."

*God, I want to take Your initiative in situations and act responsibly.* ■

# *The Peter Pan Syndrome*

**REFLECT**

In what areas of your life do you still wish for magical help from someone like a Wendy?

_____

_____

_____

**REFLECT**

What keeps you from being more responsible in that area of your life?

_____

_____

_____

> **T**hose who, having heard the word with a noble and good heart, keep it and bear fruit with patience.

LUKE 8:9–15

*Then His disciples asked Him, saying, "What does this parable mean?"*

*And He said, . . . "Now the parable is this: The seed is the word of God. Those by the wayside are the ones who hear; then the devil comes and takes away the word out of their hearts, lest they should believe and be saved. But the ones on the rock are those who, when they hear, receive the word with joy; and these have no root, who believe for a while and in time of temptation fall away.*

*"And the ones that fell among thorns are those who, when they have heard, go out and are chocked with cares, riches, and pleasures of life, and bring no fruit to maturity.*

*"But the ones that fell on the good ground are those who, having heard the word with a noble and good heart, keep it and bear fruit with patience."*

**T**he story of Peter Pan is well-known, even if you never read the book or saw the movie. It's an ageless tale that most of us have at least heard by word of mouth. A young man has a magical friend who can make him fly and do all kinds of fun things. For years I had a superficial knowledge of the story even though I had never read the book.

Then someone introduced to me the "Peter Pan Syndrome." It seems the story of Peter Pan told more than it showed on the surface. One idea that the story may illustrate is that many men just don't want to grow up. They want to remain irresponsible, especially in relationships. And to be irresponsible, they need to have a "Wendy"—a special friend who can magically cover up all their irresponsibility.

Every really good story has a point beyond the obvious. And even when we don't understand these subtle points with our conscious mind, a part of us does understand. I think that's why so much of Jesus' teaching was done through stories.

Jesus didn't explain all of his parables. Some He left for listeners to chew on and figure out on their own. The parable of the soils is one He did explain to his disciples, after He told the parable to the multitude. Perhaps He explained it to the disciples because He felt that it was too important to risk having them miss the point. Maybe He just wanted them to understand how to interpret His parables.

Either way, there is little doubt about the meaning of the parable of the soil. If we are to be considered "good soil," we will be responsible listeners and doers. After Jesus had explained the details of the parable, he added, "Therefore take heed, how you hear, for whoever has, to him more will be given, and whoever does not have, even what he seems to have will be taken from him" (Luke 8:18).

The more faithful we are in doing God's Word, the more responsibility He gives us. And that will involve growing up.

Jesus states that fruit comes with patience. In what area of your life are you in a rush to be mature?

_____

_____

_____

In what ways have you resisted God's attempts to help you mature? What do you think you are trying to avoid?

_____

_____

_____

"**Our responsibility is to God and our fellowship with Him will deepen as we mature.**"

*God, I want to mature and be a responsible listener of Your words.* ∎

# God's Economy

**REFLECT**

Describe a situation where you
acted in an immature way.

_____

_____

_____

**REFLECT**

What brought you up short and
changed you to act more mature?

_____

_____

_____

LUKE 12:42–48
*And the Lord said, "Who then is that faithful and wise
servant, whom his master will make ruler over his
household, to give them their portion of food in due sea-
son?*

*"Blessed is that servant whom his master will find
so doing when he comes. . . .*

*"But if that servant says in his heart, 'My master is
delaying his coming,' and begins to beat the menser-
vants and maidservants, and to eat and drink and be
drunk, the master of that servant will come on a day
when he is not looking for him. . . .*

*"And that servant who knew his master's will, and
did not prepare himself or do according to his will, shall
be beaten with many stripes.*

*"But he who did not know, yet committed things
worthy of stripes, shall be beaten with few. For everyone to whom much is given, from him much will be required; and to whom much has been committed, of him
they will ask the more.*

Jesus tells His disciples a parable about a
master who returns unexpectedly and
wants to see if his servants are prepared. When you
read these verses, did you feel the master was somehow tricking the servant
by not telling him when he was return-
ing? Did it seem like entrapment? Did
it raise your anxiety level? There were
many possible responses to the master's delay, but faithfulness was the response that Jesus wanted.

> **T**here were many possible
> responses to the master's
> delay, but faithfulness
> was the response that
> Jesus wanted.

Maybe you've had this experience
with your kids, or you were on the
other side of it when you were a kid.
The parents are away, and while they are away,
chaos reigns, at least until the time their return ap-
proaches. If something changed, and the parents returned early, trouble would follow, for the kids
would be "found out."

One summer we left one of our boys at home for summer school, and I returned home early and unexpectedly. At 3 A.M. a neighbor telephoned and woke me out of a sound sleep. "I can't hear your band," he yelled into the phone. "What, who is this anyway?" I asked. Then my neighbor realized that he was talking with me instead of my son. "Make sure you ask your son about his talk with the sheriff" came the answer, and the man quickly terminated the conversation.

Our neighborhood has a restriction on loud noise after 10 P.M. One night a live band was playing in our backyard. Some of the neighbors who were upset about the noise level called the sheriff, who shut down the party.

That type of behavior is typical for kids. It happens at home, at church, and at school. If no one is watching, they misbehave. We all see it as immaturity or irresponsibility. When it happens with someone who is an adult or is in leadership, it's the same thing—immaturity and irresponsibility—but the difference is that we expect more from the adult.

That's why Jesus stated the principle that "To whom much is given, from him much will be required; and to whom much has been committed, of him they will ask the more." The more responsibility we have, the more responsible we are expected to be.

**What ways are you living in expectation of the return of Christ?**

_____

_____

_____

**List some steps you could take to be more prepared for the return of Christ.**

_____

_____

_____

> **"To whom much is given, from him much will be required."**

_Lord, I want to faithfully prepare for Your return._ ■

# *Leadership*

**REFLECT**

In what ways have you resisted being some kind of leader in God's scheme of things?

_____

_____

_____

**REFLECT**

What are the reasons that you have given for resisting?

_____

_____

_____

**S**hepherd the flock of God which is among you, serving as overseers, not by constraint but willingly, not for dishonest gain but eagerly (1 Peter 5:2).

EXODUS 3:9–12

*"Now therefore, behold, the cry of the children of Israel has come to Me, and I have also seen the oppression with which the Egyptians oppress them. Come now, therefore, and I will send you to Pharaoh that you may bring My people, the children of Israel, out of Egypt."*

*But Moses said to God, "Who am I that I should go to Pharaoh, and that I should bring the children of Israel out of Egypt?"*

*So He said, "I will certainly be with you. And this shall be a sign to you that I have sent you: When you have brought the people out of Egypt, you shall serve God on this mountain."*

**W**e often think of leadership as a quality that someone either has or doesn't have. We imply that people are born with it in the statement, "He's a *born* leader." Now, it's true that some people are born leaders and seem to take charge on the playground of nursery school. But if leadership is one of the characteristics of mature, godly manhood, then it must also be something that can be learned over time.

Moses appears to be the kind of leader who matured into the role. You could almost call him a reluctant leader. As a young man, Moses was raised in the house of Pharaoh. When he killed an Egyptian, Moses was beginning to exhibit leadership skills, but then he had to disappear into the desert—for forty years. Now as a shepherd in the Midian Desert, a bush began to burn and Moses went over to investigate. God talked directly to Moses in the bush and told him that he would lead the Israelites out of Egypt. Moses didn't volunteer to be a leader nor was his personality the driving factor in God's choice. It was more that God needed someone, and picked Moses because He believed he could do the job.

Now if you were any sort of leader at all, God's hand-picked selection as the leader should have set your wheels spinning. Moses's motto should have been "Let me at it." Instead, he had the nerve to argue with God about his suitability for the task. First, he deferred based on "Who am I that I should go to Pharaoh?" When that line of reasoning didn't work, he referred to his speech handicap. God told Moses that he could take his brother Aaron along to do the speaking. Finally Moses ran out of excuses and God had His leader.

If Moses had thought life was complicated before that day, he soon learned that life after his calling became *really* complicated. But think of what he would have missed. God told His name, "Yahweh," to only one man—Moses. And all those conversations with God on the mountain top would have been missed as well. There may have been hassles with Moses' job of leadership, but his benefits were beyond description.

**What is the difference between making excuses and genuine humility?**

_____

_____

_____

**If you are called by God to be a leader, how open are you to the task?**

_____

_____

_____

"**Moses didn't volunteer to be a leader nor was his personality the driving factor in God's choice.**"

*Lord, show me how to lead and teach me the skills that I need.* ∎

# *Father-in-Law Advice*

**REFLECT**

**Where do you place your priorities?**

_____

_____

_____

**REFLECT**

**How well do you delegate at home and in your family?**

_____

_____

_____

> **T**he fear of the LORD leads to life, and he who has it will abide in satisfaction; he will not be visited with evil (Prov. 19:23).

EXODUS 18:13–17

*And so it was, on the next day, that Moses sat to judge the people; and the people stood before Moses from morning until evening.*

*So when Moses' father-in-law saw all that he did for the people, he said, "What is this thing that you are doing for the people? Why do you alone sit, and all the people stand before you from morning until evening?"*

*And Moses said to his father-in-law, "Because the people come to me to inquire of God. When they have a difficulty, they come to me, and I judge between one and another; and I make known the statutes of God and His laws."*

*So Moses' father-in-law said to him, "The thing that you do is not good."*

**A**fter Moses had accepted the job of leadership, he ran with it. It was one of his special qualities as a person. As a leader, he not only continually confronted Pharaoh, but also he made himself available to the people of Israel. Most of his day was spent listening to people's complaints against each other. Besides listening, Moses gave judgments about the disputes, taught God's ways, and instructed the people about the Lord. He held a variety of roles—judge, counselor, teacher and leader—no small task!

For a number of days Jethro, Moses' father-in-law from Midian, watched Moses and his interaction with the people. Jethro quickly saw potential problems in Moses' style of leadership. Burnout is not some twentieth-century invention—Moses was quickly headed that direction. Jethro wisely pointed out that if Moses wore himself out, he would be worthless to the people. Moses needed some additional lessons in leadership.

Jethro advised Moses to set some priorities to his leadership. Teaching God's laws to the people was going to be at the top. "Teach them the statutes and the laws," Jethro told him, "and show them the way in which they must walk and the work they must do" (Ex. 18:20). Second, Moses needed to learn another basic skill for leadership—delegation. He had to give to others the tasks that were further down on his priority list. Jethro told him to select men who feared God, loved the truth, and hated covetousness.

Then Jethro taught Moses the principle of "span of control." In order to lead, the group has to be a manageable size. He encouraged the people to be broken into groups of a thousand, groups of hundreds, groups of fifties, and groups of ten. Each level would have leaders.

Lastly, Jethro taught Moses that good leaders know how to listen. Moses could see the wisdom in the counsel of Jethro. "So Moses heeded the voice of his father-in-law and did all that he had said" (Ex. 18:24). As he acquired new leadership skills, Moses avoided wearing himself out, and the people were managed with greater skill. As the top leader in the nation of Israel, Moses still got involved in judging the cases of the people—except now he only got the tough cases. He was the Israelites' Supreme Court. Moses learned some solid lessons from his father-in-law that carried him through forty years of leadership with the Israelites.

*God, thank You that we can learn principles of leadership from the example of Moses.* ∎

**REFLECT**

How well do you manage your family?

_____

_____

_____

**REFLECT**

Listening is critical. How do you and your family evaluate your listening skills?

_____

_____

_____

**"Burnout is not some twentieth-century invention—Moses was quickly headed that direction."**

# *A Servant Leader*

Name some people you know who are servant-leaders like Ezra and list the qualities that make them seem that way to you.

_____

_____

_____

**REFLECT**

What do you see that makes these people self-led?

_____

_____

_____

> **S**ervant-leadership involves knowing ourselves and being able to be a leader in our own lives first.

EZRA 7:6–10
*This Ezra came up from Babylon; and he was a skilled scribe in the Law of Moses, which the LORD God of Israel had given. The king granted him all his request, according to the hand of the LORD his God upon him. Some of the children of Israel, the priests, the Levites, the singers, the gatekeepers, and the Nethinim came up to Jerusalem in the seventh year of King Artaxerxes.*

*And Ezra came to Jerusalem in the fifth month, which was in the seventh year of the king. On the first day of the fifth month he began his journey from Babylon, and on the first day of the fifth month he came to Jerusalem, according to the good hand of his God upon him.*

*For Ezra had prepared his heart to seek the Law of the LORD, and to do it, and to teach statutes and ordinances in Israel.*

**C**yrus, King of Persia, had overthrown the Babylonians and, in doing so, inherited the Jews, who had been conquered by the Babylonians. He was interested in the Jews rebuilding Jerusalem, and in particular, rebuilding the Temple. Their efforts to rebuild the Temple were discouraged by their enemies around Jerusalem, so the work stopped. When Darius followed Cyrus as King of Persia, he ordered the work completed and the Temple was finished.

More than fifty years later, Ezra arrived in Jerusalem, and was shocked to find that, although the Temple was there, the people knew little of what it meant to follow the Lord (see Ezra 9). The work had been finished externally; they had restored the Temple. But the real work was internal, and Ezra began the work of rebuilding the hearts of the people.

Leadership that focuses on external issues is difficult, but the type of leadership that concerns the matters of the heart is what makes for godly masculinity. Ezra provided that leadership. He led by being a servant himself. He wept and prayed for his people, and led them through his own humility and confession.

Most of contemporary thinking about what it means to lead involves taking charge and motivating people. Ezra showed us a different type of leadership. First of all, he took charge of his own life by preparing "his heart to seek the Law of the Lord, and to do it." Then out of his knowing and doing, he was prepared to teach and lead the people.

In three different churches, I have worked with pastors who had three different styles of leadership. One of the pastors was only concerned with the externals of leadership—buildings. His leadership was exhibited in grand church buildings. Another one of the pastors didn't give the outside much thought but was constantly building the lives of people. Finally, I worked with a third pastor who had learned to balance between a concern for the external building and the internal relationship with the heart of the people. Servant leadership means that we should first be led by the Lord and then we can attempt to lead.

**REFLECT**

Who are some people you know who try to lead others, but know little about being self-led?

_____

_____

_____

**REFLECT**

Describe some areas of your life where you are self-led.

_____

_____

_____

*Lord, teach me how to be a servant leader.* ■

"**They had restored the Temple, but the real work was internal. Ezra began the work of rebuilding the hearts of the people.**"

# A Leader's Sacrifice

**REFLECT**

How much do you sacrifice your comforts in the positions of leadership God has placed you in?

_____

_____

_____

**REFLECT**

Where in your life do you struggle most with being a sacrificial leader?

_____

_____

_____

Jesus said, "But go and learn what this means: 'I desire mercy and not sacrifice.' For I did not come to call the righteous, but sinners, to repentance (Matt. 9:13).

NEHEMIAH 7:1–4

*Then it was, when the wall was built and I had hung the doors, when the gatekeepers, the singers, and the Levites had been appointed, that I gave the charge of Jerusalem to my brother Hanani, and Hananiah the leader of the citadel, for he was a faithful man and feared God more than many.*

*And I said to them, "Do not let the gates of Jerusalem be opened until the sun is hot; and while they stand guard, let them shut the doors and bar them; and appoint guards from among the inhabitants of Jerusalem, one at his watch station and another in front of his own house."*

*Now the city was large and spacious, but the people in it were few, and the houses were not rebuilt.*

**N**ehemiah was prepared internally for what God was calling him to do in Jerusalem. Although he was very different in temperament from Ezra, a priest, God used their differences to accomplish His purposes in rebuilding the city. That's because on the inside, they both were leaders of themselves first.

Nehemiah had a position of power and comfort in Persia. But he was not possessed by those comforts. He was a man who was possessed only by his passion for godliness and faithfulness. And his leadership skills were needed in Jerusalem.

Nehemiah demonstrated more of what we typically define as leadership. He was able to plan carefully not only what needed to be done, but how to do it. He motivated people to work as a team. When problems arose, he solved them and encouraged his workers.

But note some additional characteristics. He was one of the workers. He didn't lead from some comfortable office, he led from the front lines. When the workers' lives were threatened, Nehemiah's life was on the line as well. Working alongside the people, Nehemiah showed us a clear picture of servant-leadership. But he also showed us that godly leaders know how to sacrifice their own comforts, and that their sacrificial attitude can win the hearts of the people.

One of my pastor friends leads one of the largest churches in Southern California with a number of associate pastors. Recently a toilet in the men's bathroom was overflowing. As the water gushed out on the floor, a group of the associate pastors gathered, wondering what to do. Then the senior pastor marched into the bathroom, shoved his sleeve up, and reached into the gushing toilet. He pulled whatever was clogging it out and resolved the incident. This pastor had learned the principles of servant leadership. Like Nehemiah, he was not afraid to lead through a sacrificial example—even if it meant some bathroom plunging.

**Why do you think you struggle in that area?**

_____

_____

_____

**In looking at the connection between prayer and action, which is dominant in your life?**

_____

_____

_____

_____

"Godly leaders know how to sacrifice their own comforts."

*God, teach me to be a self-sacrificing leader.* ■

# The Leader of the Family

REFLECT

Describe your type of leadership in your home. Are you a servant-leader or a sacrificing leader?

_____

_____

_____

REFLECT

In what ways are you connecting with your family's generations to come?

_____

_____

_____

> **If first we are "self-leaders," and then we are "family-leaders," the other areas requiring leadership become much easier.**

GENESIS 24:1–6
*Now Abraham was old, well advanced in age; and the LORD had blessed Abraham in all things. So Abraham said to the oldest servant of his house, who ruled over all that he had, "Please, put your hand under my thigh, and I will make you swear by the LORD, the God of heaven and the God of the earth, that you will not take a wife for my son from the daughters of the Canaanites, among whom I dwell; but you shall go to my country and to my kindred, and take a wife for my son Isaac."*

*And the servant said, "Perhaps the woman will not be willing to follow me to this land. Must I take your son back to the land from which you came?"*

*But Abraham said to him, "Beware that you do not take my son back there."*

I've always enjoyed reading about Abraham. But as I read through his life, I often wonder why a whole chapter is devoted to the account of how Abraham found a wife for his son Isaac to marry. I believe it contains leadership principles for the family.

Sometimes we may look at Abraham's life when Sarah was alive and wonder who really was in charge—Sarah or Abraham. Our answer many times would have to be Sarah. She certainly was in charge when she ordered Abraham to get rid of Ishmael and Hagar.

In this story, Abraham was an old man, preparing to die. He had remarried, so he had a wife. And he had other children by that wife, but his focus was on the child of promise. As the family patriarch, Abraham took seriously his leadership role within the family to make certain the family connections were going to be right. He was concerned about what would happen when he was gone. Abraham knew that it was important to get Isaac a wife from his relatives in Mesopotamia, but Abraham didn't want the servant to take his son back to the land of his fathers. So to pre-serve his leadership in future generations, Abraham sent his servant back to Mesopotamia on a mission to get Isaac a bride.

Being a servant-leader in our families is probably the most difficult form of leadership we can experience as men. It is not simply a matter of resolving the question of who submits. It is involved with the generations. It means we are involved with our children. We are their friends and their mentors to some extent. We are connected to them and contribute to their lives. Being a leader at home means taking the initiative, rather than waiting for our wives or someone else to chart the course for us.

Sometimes when my younger son and I would be involved in a heated discussion, my wife would jump into the situation to protect our son. I remember asking her to let my son and I work it out. At first, it was extremely difficult for her to handle these conversations and sometimes she had to leave the room. But she did follow through and leave the room. And my son and I both survived. In fact, through these discussions, we built a strong relationship that I pray will affect the generations to come in my family. That's what family leadership is about according to Abraham.

 **REFLECT**

How are you leading the next generations?

_____

_____

 **REFLECT**

What are some of the obstacles to your being a family leader?

_____

_____

_____

>  "**Being a leader at home means taking the initiative.**"

*Lord, give me the courage to lead in my family.* ■

# *A Leader at Home*

**REFLECT**

How do your family or friends react when you relate the great things the Lord has done for you?

_____

_____

_____

**REFLECT**

How do you respond when the reaction of others is different from what you expected?

_____

_____

_____

**S**ervant leadership is demonstrated as we share the great things God is doing in our lives with those we love.

MARK 5:15–20
*Then they came to Jesus, and saw the one who had been demon-possessed and had the legion, sitting and clothed and in his right mind. And they were afraid. And those who saw it told them how it happened to him who had been demon-possessed and about the swine.*

*Then they began to plead with Him to depart from their region. And when He got into the boat, he who had been demon-possessed begged Him that he might be with Him.*

*However, Jesus did not permit him, but said to him, "Go home to your friends, and tell them what great things the Lord has done for you, and how He has had compassion on you."*

**W**hen Jesus healed the demon-possessed man, there were several interesting reactions. Even though Mark doesn't tell us about them, we can imagine how angry the owners of the pigs were. Jesus had cast the legion of demons into a herd of swine and then the swine had plunged over a cliff and drowned in the sea. And then there was the reaction of the people who lived there to the incredible change that took place in the crazy man. The demon-possessed man was so strong the people were unable to control him, even with shackles and chains. He lived in the cemetery, and was quite a spectacle as he cut himself and hollered and screamed all the time. You'd think the people would be happy that their local "crazy" was now sane.

What were they afraid of? Were they afraid that the change was only temporary? I think they were afraid of Jesus, for he had tamed what no one there could tame. The Lord Jesus had a power that was beyond anything they had ever seen before. No wonder the man didn't want to stay around that crowd. Who knew what they would do after Jesus left in the boat.

The other interesting reaction to Jesus is the man's request to go with the Savior. Instead of His usual statement that no one was to be told, Jesus said to this man, "Go home to your friends, and tell them what great things the Lord has done for you." Obviously Jesus had a reason for what He did. Perhaps He knew the potential leadership abilities this man had as well as the healing that needed to take place with his family and friends. When the people learned about what Jesus had done for the man, the Scriptures say they "all marveled."

Being a leader at home is the true test of leadership, especially when we understand biblical leadership as being servant-leadership. I know people who have been effective leaders in the community but their homes are disasters—their kids are out of control, their wife is angry, and they have given up on leadership and buried themselves in their work. I see leaders like this in my counseling practice. They have learned principles of leadership in the business world but don't think of using the exact same qualities in their home. As a result, they are missing something on the inside.

To exercise this type of servant-leadership at home, we don't have to be the father. Even a single young man can begin with self-leadership. I've learned that it takes a greater strength to lead at home than in the church or the office.

**How do you get yourself back on course?**

_____

_____

_____

**Plan some steps to demonstrate servant-leadership in your home.**

_____

_____

_____

>
> **"Being a leader at home is the true test of leadership."**

*Lord, help me to talk about your presence in my life with my family.* ■

# Leadership in Worship

**REFLECT**

How much of a leadership role do
you take in spiritual worship? Describe what you do.

_____

_____

_____

**REFLECT**

How do you express the emotional
side of worship?

_____

_____

_____

2 SAMUEL 6:18, 20–23

*And when David had finished offering burnt offerings
and peace offerings, he blessed the people in the name of
the LORD of hosts. . . .*

*Then David returned to bless his household. And
Michal the daughter of Saul came out to meet David,
and said, "How glorious was the king of Israel today,
uncovering himself today in the eyes of the maids of his
servants, as one of the base fellows shamelessly uncov-
ers himself!"*

*So David said to Michal, "It was before the LORD,
who chose me instead of your father and all his house,
to appoint me ruler over the people of the LORD, over Israel. Therefore I will play music before the LORD. And I
will be even more undignified than this, and will be
humble in my own sight. But as for the maidservants of
whom you have spoken, by them I will be held in
honor."*

*Therefore Michal the daughter of Saul had no chil-
dren to the day of her death.*

In the Bible, spiritual leadership is placed in
the hands of men, but in practice, most spiritual leadership outside of the pulpit is done by
women. They hold the Bible studies, teach the children, and enjoy the experience of worship. Somehow we don't think of spirituality as
being a manly quality. Perhaps that has
taken place because worship and spirituality involve the emotions, and the emotions are still considered feminine by
most men in our culture.

> **In traditional Jewish worship, public worship is men's work.**

Not only is that counter to what we see
in Scripture, it also goes against what we see in other
cultures. In traditional Jewish worship, as well as in
Islam and Buddhism, public worship is men's work.
They do the public prayers and worship. Whatever
the woman experiences is done through the men in
her family.

Perhaps that's why David's wife, Michal, was home on the day they celebrated the return of the ark of the Lord to Jerusalem. David organized and led the procession that must have taken forever to get where it was going. Every six steps, they stopped and offered a sacrifice. And there was no lack of enthusiasm on this trip as "David danced before the Lord with all his might"!

In David's case, it was Michal who tried to put a wet blanket on the worship experience. In our day, we men often are the wet blanket that tries to dampen the emotional enthusiasm centered around worship. "Let's not get carried away," might be the modern version of what Michal said to David. Our lack of enthusiasm may be related to our fear of too much emotion, but we need to be careful we don't worry so much about the outward appearance that we lose our hearts.

In what ways have you observed people like Michal who are more concerned with outward appearance in their worship?

_____

_____

_____

How do you avoid an absorbing concern with the outward appearance of worship?

_____

_____

_____

**"We cannot be really comfortable with our manhood until we are comfortable as men in our worship."**

*Lord, I want to be able to express the emotional side of worship.* ■

# *Taking Risks*

**REFLECT**

How willing am I to risk—no matter whether I succeed or fail?

_____

_____

_____

**REFLECT**

How does my fear limit me?

_____

_____

_____

> **T**he key question isn't how many talents we've been given, but rather how we are investing them.

MATTHEW 25:19–23

*"After a long time the lord of those servants came and settled accounts with them. So he who had received five talents came and brought five other talents, saying, 'Lord, you delivered to me five talents; look, I have gained five more talents besides them.'*

*"His lord said to him, 'Well done, good and faithful servant; you were faithful over a few things, I will make you ruler over many things. Enter into the joy of your lord.'*

*"He also who had received two talents came and said, 'Lord, you delivered to me two talents; look, I have gained two more talents besides them.'*

*"His lord said to him, 'Well done, good and faithful servant; you have been faithful over a few things, I will make you ruler over many things. Enter into the joy of your Lord.'"*

**A**nother important trait of godly masculinity is the ability to take proper risks. We're not talking necessarily about taking risks in the stock market or in a race car. The men who take these risks often interpret them as signs of their manhood. But in the biblical economy, taking risks is the ability to fail or to lose all and still feel a sense of integrity.

In the parable of the talents, two men had the courage to risk and if you read the rest of the parable (Matt. 25:24–30), you'll learn about the one man who didn't risk anything. This man buried his one talent into the ground and so returned it to the master in exactly the condition that it was given. The man who would not risk ended up losing everything. I wonder what would have happened if the man who was given two talents had made a bad deal and lost everything. How would the master have reacted?

Perhaps the reaction of the master would depend on what kind of risks the man took. If he was careless, he may have suffered the same judgment as the man who took no risks. But if he had acted carefully and then suffered a setback, I believe Jesus would have somehow found a way to honor that kind of strength.

Taking the right kind of risks means that I jump into life with both feet. If I don't take any risks, it means that I only have one foot in life, and in some significant way, I am still holding back. It reminds me of the lukewarm churches that Jesus was so angry about in the third chapter of the Book of Revelation.

A number of years ago, I worked for a book publisher as an acquisitions editor. I was about ready to begin my counseling practice but I had a limited base of people. For a while I worked both jobs with one foot in my counseling practice, but in another way, I was holding back and working my editor position. Finally, I reached a point at which I had to devote all my time to my counseling practice. It was scary for me to put my neck on the line like this—but my risk was rewarded and my practice took off.

I like the word *talents* in this parable because it goes beyond the idea of money. Each of us have been given talents, to some degree. The key question isn't how many talents we've been given but rather how we are investing them. Not to risk at all is to risk losing all.

**REFLECT**

Describe a situation in which you played it so safe you really missed the opportunity. What were you protecting?

_____

_____

_____

**REFLECT**

Describe areas of your life where you do take risks. What is different about those areas and those where you don't take risks?

_____

_____

_____

" **Sometimes the biggest risk is not to take a risk.** "

*Lord, thank You for the talents You've given me. Help me to use them wisely.* ■

# *Standing Firm*

**REFLECT**

Describe the results of a time when you have pressed a point with an authority figure.

_____

_____

_____

**REFLECT**

Consider some of the authority figures in your life now and what the risk would be if you were to take a strong stand with them.

_____

_____

_____

GENESIS 18:22–26

*. . . Abraham still stood before the LORD. And Abraham came near and said, "Would You also destroy the righteous with the wicked? Suppose there were fifty righteous within the city; would You also destroy the place and not spare it for the fifty righteous that were in it?*

*"Far be it from You to do such a thing as this, to slay the righteous with the wicked, so that the righteous should be as the wicked; far be it from You! Shall not the Judge of all the earth do right?"*

*And the LORD said, "If I find in Sodom fifty righteous within the city, then I will spare all the place for their sakes."*

**H**ave you ever been in one of these situations: When you ask for something, you get it and then realize that if you had asked for more, you would have gotten that as well?

One of my hobbies is collecting old fountain pens. Once I got a catalog with color pictures of a group of pens in Switzerland. It was a silent auction, so I faxed my bid to the auction several days ahead of time. I really liked an old Pelican German pen from the 1930s. When I received notice that I had successfully bid on that particular pen, I wondered if I had paid too much. Since I was miles away from the auction, I never did know and had to be content that I received what I wanted.

Abraham didn't fax his bid to God. He and God had a conversation about how many righteous men would have to be found in the city of Sodom so that God wouldn't destroy the city. Abraham started the bidding at fifty. "Suppose there were fifty righteous within the city; would You also destroy the place?" Abraham asked. When God said He would spare the city for fifty people, Abraham took a risk. Should he

> **T**he father of the Israelites dared to stand firm before God and press for everything he felt he could.

bargain with God? Why not? So he asked for forty-five; then forty; and so on until he reached ten. When God said He would spare the city for ten, Abraham felt that he had taken the conversation as far as he could; then he accepted the results of his bargaining.

It's risking to bargain with any authority figure, let alone the Creator of the universe. But there was a key character trait in Abraham that was similar to his later descendant Moses. Abraham cared about people and knew that God cared about the people of Sodom even more than he did. So the father of the Israelites dared to stand firm before God and press for everything he felt he could.

Was it presumptive to bargain with God over the fate of the people in Sodom? I don't think so, because God stayed in the bargaining process with Abraham. Sometimes we do ask with a presumptive attitude as if we know better than God. To press his point and ask repeatedly, Abraham took a risk, but he rested in the knowledge that God was God. If God had said, "Enough already," Abraham would have conceded, confident that his risk had been honored by God.

**REFLECT**

How do you press a point with God in prayer without becoming presumptive and assuming that you know better than God?

_____

_____

_____

**REFLECT**

How do you avoid being passive when you should be pressing the point?

_____

_____

_____

"We must be able to find the balance between being presumptive and being passive."

*Lord, give me a sense of balance in my life for to-day.* ■

# *Risking Death by Fire*

**REFLECT**

Describe a time when have you taken a risk because of your faith in God and your desire to be obedient to him.

_____

_____

_____

**REFLECT**

There is no guarantee of a miracle simply because we risk everything in obedience. When have you been disappointed after risking because of your faith?

_____

_____

_____

> **W**e need to take the risk and obey God regardless of our circumstances.

DANIEL 3:19–21, 24–25
*Then Nebuchadnezzar was full of fury, and the expression on his face changed toward Shadrach, Meshach, and Abed-Nego. Therefore he spoke and commanded that they heat the furnace seven times more than it was usually heated. And he commanded certain mighty men of valor who were in his army to bind Shadrach, Meshach, and Abed-Nego, and cast them into the burning fiery furnace.*

*Then these men were bound in their coats, their trousers, their turbans, and their other garments, and were cast into the midst of the burning fiery furnace. . . .*

*Then King Nebuchadnezzar was astonished; and he rose in haste and spoke, saying to his counselors, "Did we not cast three men bound into the midst of the fire?" They answered and said to the king, "True, O king."*

*"Look!" he answered, "I see four men loose, walking in the midst of the fire; and they are not hurt, and the form of the fourth is like the Son of God."*

**E**veryone has heard of Daniel's three friends, Shadrach, Meshach, and "To-bed-we-go"— at least that's how I learned their names as a kid. I remember the awe we felt in that Sunday school class when we heard the story of them being tossed into the fiery furnace. What our teacher didn't tell us was the extent of the violence from King Nebuchadnezzar. When people didn't do exactly as the king commanded, he made Darth Vader look mild.

When Zedekiah, king of Israel, rebelled against Nebuchadnezzar, he was blinded as punishment (see 2 Kings 25). But the cruel Nebuchadnezzar had a special treat for him just prior to that vicious act. He had him watch his sons be killed, probably in some gruesome way, making that the last image Zedekiah ever saw. Nebuchadnezzar wasn't to be messed with.

So how did these young men who worked for Nebuchanezzar's government ever find the courage to openly disobey him? Did they have a death wish? Was their faith bordering on being presumptive? Not really, for these men were clearly choosing to obey one of God's important laws, and were willing to die rather than disobey.

When Nebuchadnezzar heard what they had done, he gave them one last chance, and then, to make an example of them, had them bound and tossed into the fiery furnace. The furnace was so hot, the men who threw them inside also lost their lives. Yet the only thing that burned on these three men were the ropes that bound them.

One of the lessons from this story is that we need to take the risk and obey God regardless of our circumstances. Then we give God the opportunity to work wonders in our lives. True freedom is found when we risk everything in obedience to God.

 **REFLECT**

How have you handled that disappointment?

_____
_____
_____

 **REFLECT**

Describe places where you need to be more willing to take calculated risks for the Lord. What support do you need?

_____
_____
_____

> **"True freedom is found when we risk everything to be obedient to God."**

*Lord, give me the courage to risk in obedience to You.* ■

# The Opportunity to Risk All

**REFLECT**

You've seen friends take risks which were unnecessary. How do you define an unnecessary risk?

_____

_____

_____

**REFLECT**

Describe some unnecessary risks you have taken.

_____

_____

_____

DANIEL 6:19–23

*Then the king arose very early in the morning and went in haste to the den of lions.*

*And when he came to the den, he cried out with a lamenting voice to Daniel. The king spoke, saying to Daniel, "Daniel, servant of the living God, has your God, whom you serve continually, been able to deliver you from the lions?"*

*Then Daniel said to the king, "O king, live forever! My God sent His angel and shut the lions' mouths, so that they have not hurt me, because I was found innocent before Him; and also, O king, I have done no wrong before you."*

*Then the king was exceedingly glad for him. . . . So Daniel was taken up out of the den, and no injury whatever was found on him, because he believed in his God.*

**Y**esterday, when we read about the three young men in the fiery furnace, did you notice that Daniel wasn't in the group? Although these young men were together in Babylon, in the opening pages of Daniel, the Scriptures don't tell us why Daniel wasn't mentioned. Perhaps he was too young and too inconspicuous to have been noticed. We can be certain from the other things we read about Daniel that he had faithfully followed the Lord in the same way as Shadrach and his friends.

As the years passed, Daniel rose in power within the government. When the Medes conquered Babylon, the new king, Darius, made him one of his top three administrators.

Not everyone was happy with Daniel's success, nor were they happy with the friendship that seemed to grow between Darius and Daniel. When Daniel was tossed into the lion's den, he was eighty years old. You wouldn't think that Darius would see Daniel as a threat to anyone. Perhaps Daniel didn't

> **G**odly risk-taking represents a continuation of a pattern of faith in the face of new opposition.

see his relationship with the king as any threat to the king's power. Besides, for quite a long time, his life as a Jew in Babylon had gone quite smoothly.

Have you ever had the feeling when things are going along nicely that the other shoe is about to drop? If Daniel hadn't thought of that possibility earlier, he certainly started thinking about it when some of his fellow administrators got Darius to sign a new law. The law made it wrong to ask anyone, including God, for anything during the next thirty days. That virtually outlawed prayer. Yet it sounded innocent enough to King Darius. He didn't realize how he'd been set up against his friend Daniel until it was too late.

Daniel was a genuine man. He personified a godly masculinity, which included taking risks based on his faith in God. Darius' new law didn't faze Daniel at all. As always, he continued to pray. Like his friends some sixty years earlier, Daniel risked his life in obedience to God. And like those three young men, God miraculously delivered him from the lions' den.

These Jewish men didn't take the risks for the thrill of it. They risked all for their faith. Both Nebuchadnezzar and Darius turned toward heaven and recognized the living God in these incidents. The turning point for these kings came from Daniel and his friends' risky devotion to God.

*Lord, show me the difference between a godly risk and an unnecessary risk.* ■

**What do you think was your motivation and the motivation of others to take these unnecessary risks?**

_____

_____

_____

**How would you counsel your son, or close friend, to differentiate between godly risk and unnecessary risk?**

_____

_____

_____

> **"These Jewish men didn't take the risks for the thrill of it. They risked all for their faith."**

# *Stand or Run?*

**Describe an experience where you have experienced God's power in your life.**

_____

_____

_____

**Sometimes we meet people who are obnoxious, but who claim their behavior is done in the name of God. To us, it is obvious that the power of God is not at work within them. When have you experienced this with someone else?**

_____

_____

_____

> **When risk-taking is empowered by the power of God, it is not really a risk.**

ACTS 5:19–23, 25

*At night an angel of the Lord opened the prison doors and brought them out, and said, "Go, stand in the temple and speak to the people all the words of this life."*

*And when they heard that, they entered the temple early in the morning and taught. But the high priest and those with him came and called the council together, with all the elders of the children of Israel, and sent to the prison to have them brought.*

*But when the officers came and did not find them in the prison, they returned and reported, saying, "Indeed we found the prison shut securely, and the guards standing outside before the doors; but when we opened them, we found no one inside!"*

*. . . . Then one came and told them, saying, "Look, the men whom you put in prison are standing in the temple and teaching the people!"*

Often we are tempted to be too quick about putting halos on the heads of the characters we meet on the pages of Scripture. We forget that they were as human as we are, and that fear was as much a part of their experience as it is ours. Knowing their fear gives an amazing twist to this story about Peter and the other apostles.

The powerful religious leaders reacted with jealousy to the apostles' preaching and threw them into jail. Before morning, an angel of the Lord came and released them, and commanded them to go to the Temple and start preaching again. I think I would have rubbed my eyes a couple of times and found some way to get out of town. But I would have missed all the excitement.

It's almost humorous to read about how the religious leaders had a hard time figuring out what to do. First there was the mystery of alert guards and the locked prison doors, but no prisoners were inside. Then these leaders received a report that the prisoners had turned up outside the doors of the Temple and they were continuing to preach—exactly what they had been arrested for the night before.

Finally these leaders gathered their wits about themselves and began to act like leaders, though they were still somewhat confused. The captain of the officers went to the apostles and asked them to appear before the religious leaders. The captain made the request with gentleness because "they feared the people, lest they should be stoned." The crowd was obviously behind the apostles and these guards knew it.

Then the high priest reminded the apostles that they were told to stop this preaching. As if a reminder would stop the apostles at this point!

When Peter answered the high priest, he gave us a principle for taking risks in our lives. He says, "We ought to obey God rather than men." It wasn't just an act of disciplined obedience that motivated the apostles. It was nothing less than a principle for risk-taking for all time.

How did you know it was the person and not God?

_____

_____

_____

Have you ever acted obnoxious, and how did you know?

_____

_____

_____

> **"We ought to obey God rather than men."**

*Lord, give me the insight to know when You are empowering me to take a risk.* ■

# *Facing the Giant*

### REFLECT

What or who are some of the giants you have tackled in your life?

_____

_____

_____

### REFLECT

Why did you tackle them and what resulted?

_____

_____

_____

**Giants can either paralyze you, as with the Israelites in the wilderness, or they can cause you to tap into God's power and defeat them.**

1 SAMUEL 17:45–49
*Then David said to the Philistine, "You come to me with a sword, with a spear, and with a javelin. But I come to you in the name of the LORD of hosts, the God of the armies of Israel, whom you have defied.*

*"This day the LORD will deliver you into my hand, and I will strike you and take your head from you. . . . Then all this assembly shall know that the LORD does not save with sword and spear, but the battle is the LORD's, and He will give you into our hands."*

*And it was so, when the Philistine arose and came and drew near to meet David, that David hastened and ran toward the army to meet the Philistine. Then David put his hand in his bag and took out a stone; and he slung it and struck the Philistine in his forehead, so that the stone sank into his forehead, and he fell on his face to the earth.*

If Goliath were on a basketball team, they would have an instant winner. All he needed to do was put his almost ten-foot frame beside the basket and wait for a pass. He wouldn't even have to jump to put the ball through the hoop. But Goliath wasn't a basketball player, he was a warrior. And he was awesome! His armor weighed more than most of the men in the Israeli army. And he was challenging them to send anyone to fight him.

It was certainly an efficient way to fight a battle, especially if you had a Goliath. With one face off, the battle would be settled and the casualties would only total one. The Philistines probably had quite a winning streak going since Goliath enlisted. After all, Saul was the tallest man in Israel, and he was no match for Goliath in size. Saul and his army knew they could not match the strength of Goliath and they were paralyzed. No one was willing to risk not the life of everyone in Israel. Have you ever wondered what Saul was thinking when he permitted David to go out there to meet Goliath? He might have laughed as David tried on his armor, except that the situation was too serious for jokes. Did Saul have a flashback to the days of old, when God gave Saul victory? Or was he willing to sacrifice this young kid and then claim to the Philistines that he didn't send him to represent the army? My guess is that David stirred up old memories of what God had done for Israel in the past. And in a moment of reflection he agreed to let David fight. David took a risk of faith in obedience to God. When our faith is clear, we can minimize the risk. But it is still a risk of faith nonetheless.

In this story, the risks were not just with David—all of Israel was at risk. That is, unless they remembered the principle that there is no risk when we are obedient to God's calling.

**REFLECT**

Who or what are some of the giants challenging you today?

_____

_____

_____

**REFLECT**

What steps can you take to begin to challenge these giants?

_____

_____

_____

"**There is no risk when we are obedient to God's calling.**"

*Lord, I want to tackle the giants in my life in Your power and strength.* ∎

# Ready to Die, Ready to Live

**REFLECT**

In the honesty of your own heart, how comfortable are you with your own death? Obviously, we're not talking about death-wishes. We're talking about having already faced the reality of your own death and accepting it the way Paul did.

_____

_____

_____

**REFLECT**

If today were the day you died, what would you do differently today (Apart from staying home from work!)?

_____

_____

_____

**F**or if we believe that Jesus died and rose again, even so God will bring with Him those who sleep in Jesus (1 Thess. 4:14).

PHILIPPIANS 1:27–28, 2:1
_Only let your conduct be worthy of the gospel of Christ, so that whether I come and see you or am absent, I may hear of your affairs, that you stand fast in one spirit, with one mind striving together for the faith of the gospel, and not in any way terrified by your adversaries, which is to them a proof of perdition, but to you of salvation, and that from God._

_Therefore if there is any consolation in Christ, if any comfort of love, if any fellowship of the Spirit, if any affection and mercy, fulfill my joy by being like-minded, having the same love, being of one accord, of one mind._

**T**he story is told that a great samurai challenged a Japanese man to battle because the man had offended him. The Japanese man served ceremonial tea for a living and to prepare himself, he asked another samurai what he should do. "What do you do best?" his teacher asked him.

"I serve tea," the man answered.

"Then accept that tomorrow is the day you die and before you die, serve your opponent tea the best you know how." He wasn't being a fatalist. That's how the samurai lived—by accepting that "Today is the day I die," and then living that day as if it were the last.

One can see the freedom and the confidence that results from such a perspective. There would be no fear, for one has faced the biggest fear, death, and in conquering that fear one can now fully live.

The Apostle Paul spelled out the same principle as the secret to his way of living boldly, regardless of the circumstances. Paul was not afraid of death. He saw it as a stepping stone from this life to the presence of Jesus, his Lord. Because he was ready to die, in every sense of the word, he was free to risk all for the sake of the gospel.

It's much easier to talk about than to do. When it comes to saying what Paul wrote to the Philippians, I may be able to say the words, and even understand and accept their meaning in a spiritual sense, but I'm not at all sure I feel the same as Paul did. Most of us don't like to talk about death. It's a subject that we pass through our experience when we must attend a funeral of a loved one, or when someone in our circle of family and friends is facing a terminal illness. Otherwise, the topic is far removed from us and doesn't touch our daily lives and experience. What if we lived our daily lives with that sort of expectancy? For me, I love life and I'm just not that relaxed when I think about dying. That must also mean that I'm not quite as bold about living either. The two attitudes go together. As I am comfortable about my future and my place in the presence of Christ, I can gain a new boldness in my daily decisions and living.

 **REFLECT**

Describe three things you will begin to do differently because you have accepted the fact that at any moment you could be gone from here and present with the Lord.

_____

_____

 **REFLECT**

Solidify your plans to change by talking it over with a friend or family member.

_____

_____

_____

**"If I can accept that today I may die, I can live this day boldly."**

*God, give me the boldness to live every day for You.* ■

# *Finishing Strong*

**REFLECT**

Where do you feel you have failed in either being true to yourself or to God?

_____

_____

_____

**REFLECT**

Unforgiveness is often connected to our continuing sense of failure. In what ways are you controlled by unforgiveness?

_____

_____

_____

> **W**e can redeem the past by trusting completely in God's grace and power.

JUDGES 16:28–31

*Then Samson called to the LORD, saying, "O LORD God, remember me, I pray! Strengthen me, I pray, just this once, O God, that I may with one blow take vengeance on the Philistines for my two eyes!"*

*And Samson took hold of the two middle pillars which supported the temple, and he braced himself against them, one on his right and the other on his left.*

*Then Samson said, "Let me die with the Philistines!" And he pushed with all his might, and the temple fell on the lords and all the people who were in it. So the dead that he killed at his death were more than he had killed in his life.*

*And his brothers and all his father's household came down and took him, and brought him up and buried him between Zorah and Eshtaol in the tomb of his father Manoah. He had judged Israel for twenty years.*

**S**amson was full of potential as a leader. Who knows what he might have accomplished if he hadn't messed up his life. Apparently Samson never outgrew the adolescent period of life in which everything about the person is proven sexually. For all of his mighty strength, he melted around women, especially those he knew he shouldn't trust.

On the surface, Samson had everything going for him. He had good parents and from birth he was set apart to be a leader in Israel, "to deliver Israel out of the hand of the Philistines" (Judges 13:5).

During his life, Samson had many ups and downs. He had a Philistine wife and during the marriage feast, his wife was given to his best man. Later Samson singlehandedly attacked and killed many Philistines.

Then Samson fell in love with Delilah. Ultimately she tricked Samson into telling the secret of his strength by having a man cut Samson's hair while he was sleeping. When the Philistines captured this mighty man who was instantly weak, they put out his eyes and made him a grinder in their prison. We usually think of Samson as a failure. And while Samson failed in many ways, he still made the list of heroes of the faith in Hebrews 11. There he is not remembered for his strength, or even his failures. He is noted as one who through faith trusted God.

We often remind ourselves that first impressions count, and that is true. Yet there's something more important about how we finish. Samson's end was the beginning of what God had promised He would accomplish through Samson—the Lord started the rescue of Israel from the Philistines. When Samson pushed over the main pillars of the temple that was full of Philistines, more people died at the time of Samson's death than when he was alive. In death, he accomplished what he failed to do in life.

One of the things we learn from Samson is that it's never too late to start over. We may be struggling with our own failures and our own sense of failure, but the story of Samson reminds us that godly men never quit. And God never gives up, either.

*God, thank You that it is never too late to start over.* ■

Whom do you need to forgive?

_____

_____

_____

Do you need to forgive yourself so you can start over again? Try to do that today.

_____

_____

_____

> "**While Samson failed in many ways, he still made the list of heroes of the faith in Hebrews 11.**"

# *Be A Man*

**REFLECT**

In what ways have you attempted to prove to your father that you are a man?

_____

_____

_____

**REFLECT**

How is this matter of proving your manhood still an issue within you?

_____

_____

_____

> **T**herefore give your servant an understanding heart to judge your people, that I may discern between good and evil.

1 KINGS 3:5–10

*At Gibeon the LORD appeared to Solomon in a dream by night; and God said, "Ask! What shall I give you?"*

*And Solomon said: "You have shown great mercy to your servant David my father, because he walked before You in truth . . . You have continued this great kindness for him, and You have given him a son to sit on his throne, as it is this day.*

*"Now, O LORD my God, You have made Your servant king instead of my father David, but I am a little child; I do not know how to go out or come in. And Your servant is in the midst of Your people whom You have chosen. . . .*

*"Therefore give to Your servant an understanding heart to judge Your people, that I may discern between good and evil. For who is able to judge this great people of Yours?"*

*And the speech pleased the LORD, that Solomon had asked this thing.*

**T**he old story of Aladdin resurfaces from time to time and sets us all to dreaming. If only we could find a magic lamp and get the genie to offer us three wishes. Yet the old fable fades in comparison to Solomon's story. The Creator of the Universe offered Solomon anything that he wanted. Think about what you would have wanted with the opportunity.

Solomon's answer flowed from a life that was reverent. And Solomon was a man who stood in awe of the task God had given him. Rather than ask for riches, success, power, or any other tangible thing, Solomon asked for wisdom. He wanted to judge his people with discernment. Soon after his discussion with God, in which God not only granted him wisdom, but also wealth and power, Solomon awoke and realized he had been dreaming.

But then the dream of Solomon came true—just as

it did in the case of Joseph. Throughout the Bible, God often spoke through dreams. Solomon shook his head in wonder: "Was this merely a dream or has God actually spoken to me?" Instead of wrestling with the answer, Solomon got up and went to Jerusalem and worshiped God among his people.

Soon after that, two women came and asked him to decide which one would keep the baby. One baby had died during the night, and both women claimed the living baby was theirs. Solomon was the judge. Was that only a dream of a conversation with God about getting wisdom for judgment? He would soon find out. This test would tell.

Solomon's response to the dilemma has been honored for centuries. He had an idea that determined the real mother for the baby. And when he gave his answer, he knew the source of the idea—it came from God, and his people knew this, too. Solomon made a great beginning to fulfill his father's dying request that he "be strong, and prove yourself a man" (1 Kings 2:2).

Solomon apparently forgot the rest of his father's injunction to him, which was to keep the charge of the Lord and walk in His ways. What did you learn from your father about finishing your walk with the Lord?

_____

_____

_____

What are you passing on to your family about finishing your walk with the Lord?

_____

_____

_____

"God cares more about our finishing than about our stumbling."

*Lord, help me to seek wisdom from Your hand in every day decisions.* ■

# *Dying Young*

**REFLECT**

Describe someone you know who
died young but still isn't dead
enough to be buried.

_____

_____

_____

**REFLECT**

Describe someone who is fully
alive even in old age.

_____

_____

_____

> **W**e reach a point in our
> lives when we begin to
> resist stretching our-
> selves.

PSALM 92:12–15
*The righteous shall flourish like a palm tree,*
*He shall grow like a cedar in Lebanon.*
*Those who are planted in the house of the LORD*
*Shall flourish in the courts of our God.*
*They shall still bear fruit in old age;*
*They shall be fresh and flourishing,*
*To declare that the LORD is upright;*
*He is my rock, and there is no unrighteousness in Him.*

In *The Masculine Journey*, author Robert Hicks
told about the anonymous paper Dr. Howard
Hendricks passed out to his students at Dallas Theological Seminary. It was entitled, "Advice to a
(Bored) Young Man." It began, "Died, age 20; buried,
age 60. The sad epitaph of too many Americans."
Gardavsky, the Czech philosopher and martyr, said
that the greatest threat against life is not death, nor
pain, nor any other disaster. The greatest
threat is that "we might die earlier than
we really do die, before death has become
a natural necessity."

We all need to adequately fear dying
long before we are pronounced dead. It's
easy to do. We reach a point in our lives
when we begin to resist stretching ourselves. We pull back from challenge and
controversy. We avoid taking appropriate
risks. We want to enjoy the comforts we've earned.
One doesn't have to be old to feel this way. It is easy
to reach a plateau at any time in life. You stop reading any more new books or avoid any new hobby or
the idea of stretching into a new area of experience.

Our deadness can be seen in fathers who watch as

their children argue, not knowing how to take the matter in hand. It can be seen in the man who cannot make a decision because he is so afraid that it might be the wrong one. It is seen in the man who cannot take a definite stand on an issue because he doesn't believe in anything strong enough to fight for it. Such men are dead on the inside, even though they are still alive on the outside.

If you'd like to have a practical lesson in how people bear fruit in their old age, just visit a nursing home on a Sunday afternoon and see the people in their wheelchairs or stuck in front of a television set. These people are in sharp contrast to those who are in the over-sixty master's competitions. These master athletes continue to work out and train in areas like running and field and track events.

The Psalmist wrote that the righteous will "still bear fruit in old age; / They shall be fresh and flourishing" (Ps. 92:14). That's godly manhood. Are you committed to being fully alive today?

What are you doing today to make certain that you stay alive so that you can still be bearing fruit in old age?

_____

_____

_____

Plans some steps today to keep growing and active.

_____

_____

_____

**"They shall still bear fruit in old age."**

*Lord, I want to see new ways to come alive in my life.* ■

# *Alive Again*

**REFLECT**

God still brings life to deadness.
Where in your life does it feel hopeless?

_____

_____

_____

**REFLECT**

What keeps you from trusting God
to bring life in that part of you?

_____

_____

_____

GENESIS 45:25–28
*Then they went up out of Egypt, and came to the land
of Canaan to Jacob their father. And they told him, saying, "Joseph is still alive, and he is governor over all
the land of Egypt." And Jacob's heart stood still, because he did not believe them.*

*But when they told him all the words which Joseph
had said to them, and when they saw the carts which
Joseph had sent to carry him, the spirit of Jacob their father revived.*

*Then Israel said, "It is enough. Joseph my son is
still alive. I will go and see him before I die."*

**"Thus says the LORD GOD to these bones: 'Surely I will cause breath to enter into you, and you shall live'"** (Eze. 37:5).

Jacob was an old man, in years and in spirit.
Years earlier when he learned that his favorite son Joseph had been killed, it had torn him
into pieces.

Now Jacob had sent his sons into Egypt to purchase grain for the family because there was a famine in the land. The ruler in Egypt insisted that
Jacob's sons bring their younger brother, Benjamin,
on the next trip; he was the only son left
from Jacob's favorite wife, Rachel. With
reluctance, Jacob permitted Benjamin to
go with his brothers to buy grain in Egypt.

What Jacob didn't know was that in
Egypt, his son Judah was pleading with
the ruler (really their brother Joseph). Benjamin was caught with the ruler's cup inside the bag of grain. Judah wanted to
take the punishment instead of Benjamin.
He knew that if Benjamin wasn't with
them when they returned, his father
would die (Gen. 44:31). In a way, Judah
was saying that Jacob had already died on the inside,
but the absence of Benjamin would finish the job.

Perhaps you're feeling like Jacob. You've been

dead on the inside for a long time. As with the prophet Ezekiel, you look out over a valley of dry bones and you ask, "Can these bones live?" And in the life of Jacob, we see that the answer is a resounding "Yes!"

An interesting little nuance in the text says so much about Jacob. Back when Jacob had wrestled with the angel, the blessing he received was the name Israel. In that culture, a name had great significance, representing something far deeper than simply a way to identify a person in a crowd. In verse 27, we read that "the spirit of Jacob their father revived." Here, years after the wrestling match was over, Jacob was still Jacob. The blessing he received was still a long way off, but as his spirit was revived at the news that Joseph was alive, the writer refers to Jacob as Israel. He was the "blessed" man, even at this old age.

The picture we are given of Jacob in the Hebrews 11 "hall of faith" is that as "he was dying, [Jacob] blessed each of the sons of Joseph, and worshiped, leaning on the top of his staff" (Hebrews 11:21). He blessed Joseph's sons—the offspring of the son he had mourned as dead for years. And then as he worshiped God, he leaned on the staff that helped him walk on his out-of-joint hip. It was a joyous and alive moment!

Sometimes we limit God by outlining what He has to do to restore life to our deadness. What makes it hard to trust Him for that?

_____

_____

_____

Can you trust Him to do it His way and in His time?

_____

_____

_____

"**Deadness and hopelessness can be brought to life again by the God of life.**"

*God, make the deadness in my life spring to life through Your power.* ∎

# Finishing the Unfinishable

**REFLECT**

It's easy to let a failure discourage us, or cause us to give up. Describe an event where you were either tempted to give up, or actually gave up because of a failure.

_____

_____

_____

**REFLECT**

Did you recover and finish? Why or why not?

_____

_____

_____

> **Y**ou number my
>
> wanderings;
>
> **P**ut my tears in Your
>
> bottle;
>
> **A**re they not in Your
>
> book? (Ps. 56:8)

DEUTERONOMY 34:4–8

*Then the LORD said to him, "This is the land of which I swore to give Abraham, Isaac, and Jacob, saying, 'I will give it to your descendants.' I have caused you to see it with your eyes, but you shall not cross over there."*

*So Moses the servant of the LORD died there in the land of Moab, according to the word of the LORD. And He buried him in a valley in the land of Moab, opposite Beth Peor; but no one knows his grave to this day.*

*Moses was one hundred and twenty years old when he died. His eyes were not dim nor his natural vigor abated. And the children of Israel wept for Moses in the plains of Moab thirty days. So the days of weeping and mourning for Moses ended.*

God keeps track of the specifics in our lives. To the Lord of the Universe, the little things often count. In the age of grace, it is easy to forget that truth. When Jesus says God knows the number of hairs on our head, it's not to impress us with God's knowledge, but to let us know that everything matters to Him. We're told in the Psalms that God keeps a list of all our tears.

In today's Bible reading, Moses is at the end of his long life—120 years and forty years of leadership. He could have looked back and complained to God that he was being treated unfairly. When we read through Moses' life, we may think that one justifiable slip-up on his part hardly seems a good reason to keep him out of the Promised Land. The Lord allowed Moses to see the land from the top of Mount Nebo but he wasn't allowed to go into the land of milk and honey.

The angry outburst seems especially harsh when those who had caused Moses to lose his temper were still able to enter the land (see Numbers 20:1–13). To understand the reasoning behind the punishment, we need to recall a leadership principle from Jesus. To those who have been given much in the way of responsibility, much is required. Leaders will be held accountable for more. Since Moses was the leader, he understood that God's judgment on his action was fair, for more was expected of him.

Nothing in the Scripture suggests that Moses ever considered God's decision to be unfair. He never let that event pull him down and discourage him in his task. He had failed, and a consequence followed that failure. But he was a strong finisher, and he was not going to give up. So Moses finished his task with class. When everything was done, he went up to the top of Mount Nebo, from where he could see the whole Promised Land stretched out before his eyes. God gave him a "guided tour," and then Moses died a contented man. He had been faithful to the task, right up to the end!

**REFLECT**

Sometimes the hardest part is continuing when the promise of success is taken away. How do you motivate yourself to continue when you might want to quit or give up?

_____

_____

_____

**REFLECT**

Are there people to whom you can turn when you feel like quitting? List them below.

_____

_____

_____

*God, keep me faithful in finishing the task—despite the outcome.* ■

"**We are called to be faithful even though we may never know the outcome.**"

# *Pressing On*

**REFLECT**

**What are some of your God-given tasks as a man? List them.**

_____

_____

_____

**REFLECT**

**List the disciplines you need to be a strong finisher in these tasks.**

_____

_____

_____

> **Whichever race is the highest priority to me will be the one where I discipline myself.**

**1 CORINTHIANS 9:24–27**
*Do you not know that those who run in a race all run, but one receives the prize? Run in such a way that you may obtain it. And everyone who competes for the prize is temperate in all things. Now they do it to obtain a perishable crown, but we for an imperishable crown.*

*Therefore I run thus: not with uncertainty. Thus I fight: not as one who beats the air. But I discipline my body and bring it into subjection, lest, when I have preached to others, I myself should become disqualified.*

In all likelihood, Paul was finally released from prison in Rome, but then was arrested again several years later and executed some time after that. Tradition says that Paul was beheaded at a spot about three miles outside of Rome. Frederick Beuchner quotes a phrase from the apocryphal *Acts of Paul and Thecla* that describes Paul at times looking "like a man, and at times he had the face of an angel."

Beuchner goes on to say that "it was with angel eyes that he exchanged a last long glance at his executioners." He probably made certain he had the time to share his Jesus with them as well.

Paul was another strong finisher. He never stopped. He could be in prison, unwanted in a city, alone and feeling forsaken, but he was never without an opportunity to do what he loved most—to share Jesus Christ.

What kept Paul alive to the end was his determination to be God's man. Nothing was going to disqualify him from the race. We may think that such an attitude is a bit out of place in our more liberal society. But the cultures of Rome and Corinth where

Paul lived and ministered were far more liberal and perverted than ours today.

According to Paul, discipline keeps us strong when things get rough. He likened himself to a fighter or a runner who conditions himself. I enjoy watching the marathon runners in the summer Olympic games. It's amazing to watch these skilled athletes run over thirty miles at a neck-breaking pace of almost five minutes per mile. These athletes make it look so easy as they glide through the streets and tick off the miles. These athletes do not train in a haphazard manner. For each person running there have been years of road work and early runs along with a careful maintenance of diet and nutrition.

The same was true for Paul. The spreading of the Good News about Jesus Christ was central to everything right up to the end of his life. Paul wrote about finishing the race and receiving the crown, not in a competitive sense, but in the sense of staying qualified, in the sense of completing the task he had been given.

Take each of the disciplines you identified and rank them in terms of your strengths.

_____

_____

_____

What can you do to strengthen those disciplines that are weaker?

_____

_____

_____

"Run in such a way that you may obtain the prize."

God, help me to live with consistency and finish the race well. ■

# *A Willing Finisher*

This book has covered a variety of aspects of godly manhood. Consider the aspects of inner-authority and self-possession and describe your growth.

_____

_____

_____

**REFLECT**

How have you grown in facing reality and in seeing beyond physical reality to the spiritual?

_____

_____

_____

> **I**t's comforting to know in those moments of doubt that Jesus has walked the same road to manhood and has promised to walk with us in our journey.

LUKE 22:39–44

*And coming out, He went to the Mount of Olives, as He was accustomed, and His disciples also followed Him. When He came to the place, He said to them, "Pray that you may not enter into temptation."*

*And He was withdrawn from them about a stone's throw, and He knelt down and prayed, saying, "Father, if it is Your will, remove this cup from Me; nevertheless not My will, but Yours, be done."*

*Then an angel appeared to Him from heaven, strengthening Him. And being in agony, He prayed more earnestly. And His sweat became like great drops of blood falling down to the ground.*

**W**hen Jesus approached the cross, His task on earth was almost finished. In a matter of hours, He would cry from the cross, "It is finished." But in the Scripture for today, He is in the garden, praying about the task ahead of him. The immensity of that task—dying for the sins of the world—caused Jesus to sweat drops of blood as he pleaded with his Heavenly Father to find some other way.

Jesus had brought a few of His disciples with Him to the garden of Gethsemane and told them to watch and pray. Then He continued on a few feet and spent time in prayer. It seems pretty incredible that Jesus sweat drops of blood, but the journals of medicine confirm the reality of the Scriptures. It is a physiological fact that in immense agony, it is possible for someone to sweat blood.

Was Jesus pleading with the Father so He could back out of going to the cross? That's hard to imagine. The Messiah knew before He came what would be involved in our salvation. I think Jesus was simply expressing to his father the honest feelings He was having as a man. He knew that He would have to drink from a symbolic cup for the agony that he would have to endure. It was not just the agony of crucifixion, but the horror of being totally isolated from his Father during that time.

As we seek to define what it means to be a godly man, Jesus is our most perfect example of manhood. Sometimes we get so caught up in the celebration of the deity of Christ and his fulfillment of prophecy that we forget his humanity. Jesus was fully man. That means, among other things, Jesus was self-possessed with a sense of authority that came from within. He not only knew what courage was all about, Jesus knew both the material and the spiritual realities. He learned to take risks, to lead his disciples, and to act on things. And now Jesus was to be the finisher.

The writer of Hebrews referred to Jesus as the "author and finisher of our faith" (Heb. 12:2). Paul wrote that Jesus is the one "who has begun a good work in you," and "will complete it" (Phil. 1:6). We're not alone. Sometimes when you face the struggles of life, it's easy to look around the empty room and feel as if no one is there with you. The room is empty, so who cares about your difficulties? It's comforting to know in those moments of doubt that Jesus has walked the same road to manhood and has promised to walk with us in our journey.

*Jesus, help me to follow You more closely every day.* ■

**REFLECT**

How have you grown in your ability to accept responsibility and leadership?

_____

_____

_____

**REFLECT**

How have you increased your ability to take risks and finish a task?

_____

_____

_____

"**Becoming a godly man is to follow Jesus more closely.**"

# *Appendix*

## Questions for group discussion

### WEEK 1

If you are meeting together with a group of men, first personally take some time to look back over your responses to the questions during the past week. Then take some time to discuss the following questions together. Make certain that each man has opportunity to talk.

- Describe some of the ways you are like your father. Describe how you are like your mother.
- Describe some of the things you missed in your relationship with your father when you were growing up.
- Describe some of the things you treasure from your childhood relationship with your father.
- What are some of the things you vowed you would do differently when you had your own family?
- When you look back over your family, what are some of the patterns you see being repeated in your relationship with your children that you experienced in your relationship with your parents?
- What are some of the "secrets" held in your family? Talk about how you knew these were secrets.

As you discuss these things together, talk about some of your fears and concerns in being open with each other. Agree together that the things you talk about will remain confidential within the group. Take some time to pray together about your journey to deeper manhood.

### WEEK 2

Before you meet together, reflect on what you have discovered about yourself and your past this week. Then, as you meet, discuss the following questions:

- Describe your relationship with your mother, and then compare it with your relationship with your father.
- What did your mother teach you through her relationship with your dad about what it means to be a man?
- What patterns in your relationship with your parents did you want to change in your relationship with your wife and/or children?
- In what ways did your mother "mediate" your relationship with your father? Sometimes mothers "explain" the father to the son and vice versa; other times, she "interprets" the behavior of the father to the son. You may have experienced other ways your mother tried to help. Describe them.

- What is hard for you to let go of in your relationship with your parents? Are you still needing or expecting something from them?
- Describe your definition of a man.

Talk together about how you balance the four areas described in Luke 2:52 in your own life. Then take some time to share prayer requests and pray for each other.

## WEEK 3

Before you meet together, reflect on what you have discovered about yourself and your past this week. Then, as you meet, discuss the following questions:

- Discuss some of the ways you have been limited or controlled by your fears. What have been some of the consequences?
- In what ways have your fears led you to be controlled by others, even your parents, as you seek to gain their approval or keep them from thinking poorly of you?
- What are some of the things you have rebelled against and done the opposite of what was best?
- What are some of the things you have "run away" from?
- In what ways do you tend to shut down and keep people out of the vulnerable, hurting parts of your life?

As you finish your time together, make some commitments to each other to continue to be more open, allowing the other men in your group to see more of your struggle.

## WEEK 4

Before you meet together, look back over your responses to the questions this week. Then take some time together to discuss the following questions. Make certain that each man has an opportunity to talk.

- Describe some of your wounds. Who has inflicted the greatest wounds upon you? The more recent ones? The deepest ones?
- Describe how it feels to you to admit that you are weak or powerless.
- Describe the ways you have either ignored your wounds, minimized them, or made them worse.
- How has busyness kept you from facing your wounds?
- Describe what you are doing to slow down your pace of life in order to find healing for your woundedness.

As you discuss these things together, notice what is difficult for you to relate to the other men. What is difficult for you to listen to as they talk? Spend some time talking about this, and then be sure to take the time to pray for each other.

## WEEK 5

As you meet together this week, make certain you give yourself enough time to talk through this subject of grief. Work on being comfortable around emotions. When women talk emotionally, they often say very little to the other person—instead they reach out and touch them on the arm or shoulder. As in every week, it is important that each man has opportunity to talk.

- Talk about some of your losses, especially those in your relationship with your father, or lack of relationship.
- Describe some of your other losses, especially those that resulted in a sense of "loss of status," or which were very humbling.
- Describe how you have grieved over these losses. Which, if any, are unfinished?
- Are you aware of using anger as a defense against grieving in any of these experiences? What were the consequences?
- What are some of your fears related to allowing yourself permission to really grieve over some of these wounds? Describe them.
- If you have grieved through any of your losses, describe the changes that took place within you in terms of how you both saw and experienced yourself.
- Describe how you felt before, during, and after the grieving event and process.

Be certain to leave time to pray for each other. This is a critical topic and you don't want to rush your way through it.


## WEEK 6

If you have been meeting together with other men for several weeks, you are getting to know each other better, both in terms of your strengths and your wounds. As we continue in our journey, we are becoming more vulnerable, and this may seem threatening. Resist the natural tendency to draw back and skip a meeting. Instead, talk together about some of your struggles with the process.

- Describe a situation where you struggled with being obedient or with maintaining your integrity. It can either be a situation in which you failed, or one in which you succeeded.
- Talk about what made the difference between success or failure in that situation.
- What has typically made it easier for you to be obedient in the past?
- Talk about some of the things you discovered about yourself in terms of the "little things." What were some of the little things you found you needed to be more careful about in your daily life?
- When it comes to "speaking the truth in love," which have you struggled most with? Speaking the truth? Or speaking it in love?

Share some specific prayer requests with each other in relation to being truthful, obedient, or maintaining or restoring personal integrity.

## WEEK 7

As you meet together to discuss the topic of submission, avoid spending time on all the old interpretations that relate primarily to women. Instead, make certain you explore some of what struck you as new insights, and especially look at what Jesus' teachings on a submissive attitude mean in relation to manliness.

- As a man in today's competitive business environment, is it possible as a man to be "like-minded," doing nothing "through selfish ambition or conceit"?
- How do you struggle with finding the balance between pride and self-doubt? Describe examples.
- What do you struggle with as a man with the idea of "being submissive"?
- What new things are you thinking through in the relationship between manliness and sub-missiveness? What "strengths" are you finding as you consider manly submissiveness?
- Describe a recent situation that would have turned out better for you if you had been able to have a submissive spirit or an attitude of humility.

This may be a heated topic so make certain that everyone has the opportunity to talk. End on a positive note, asking each man to relate something new and practical that he will explore in relation to a "submissive attitude." Then pray specifically for each other.

## WEEK 8

A part of our week has focused on the need for us to care enough about each other that we are willing to hold each other accountable in our attitudes and behaviors. As a part of your group meeting, you might want to ask the other men if they are seeing in you some areas where you need to be more careful, or to pay closer attention. Go slowly as you begin this part of your time together so that everyone is on the same track together.

- Discuss together the areas in your life in which you are feeling discontented. How do you experience that discontentment?
- Describe some of the principles that actually guide you in:
  Your marriage
  Your family
  Your work
  Your ministry
- How can you hold each other accountable in the practicality of the principles you describe?
- Who are some of the people or situations you have difficulty saying "no" to? Discuss what makes it difficult.
- To whom are you accountable? How comfortable are you being accountable to this group?

Take some time to discuss ways you can be accountable to each other, including some of your fears and concerns about being accountable in this context. Be certain everyone expresses themselves, and, if in agreement, makes the commitment to being accountable to each other. If some are hesitant, listen to the concerns and agree to discuss it further next week. Pray for each other, both in your meeting time and throughout the week.

## WEEK 9

As your group becomes more open with each other, there may be the sense that the type of friendship we looked at this week can only come from within your group. That may or may not be true, and no one should feel any pressure to identify someone in the group as his spiritual guide or friend. Be open and honest with each other as you discuss this week's topic, giving each other the freedom to build friendship where God is directing them.

- Describe some of the men who have had a great impact on your life, both as a child, and now as an adult.
- Describe the traits these people had that made them special in your life.
- Describe an experience in which you expected more from a friendship than you were able to get. How were you hurt by that? How did you react?
- Who have been your mentors? Describe how.
- Who have been your spiritual mentors? Who is your present spiritual mentor?

Make certain that everyone has a chance to talk. Spend time talking about people who have been spiritual mentors, and then pray for each other, that each of you will find that man who can continue to be your spiritual guide on a one-to-one basis.

## WEEK 10

We've been looking at several traits of Godly masculinity this week—in particular the traits of inner confidence and a sense of authority, a decisiveness as well as a sense of being self-possessed. As you discuss the following questions, keep these traits as the focus of your discussion.

- Describe areas of your life that you still don't fully possess. How do they control you?
- How well do you know yourself? How well do you read others?
- Discuss examples of situations in which your principles set you up for conflict with your faith. Describe what God did to resolve the conflict.
- In what areas of your life are you decisive? Indecisive? Where are you able to "stick your neck out"?
- Describe your wild man. Is that part of you in control, out-of-control, or locked in a cage? How do you balance that part of you with the caring, tender part of you?
- If God offered you anything, what would you ask for? What would your second and third choices be? If He asked you to sell everything, what would you try to hold on to? Why?

As we work through the third part of this study, you will be looking at traits that are "under construction" within us. There should be no sense of failure at not possessing these traits. They represent what God wants to do within to add to our masculinity on a deeper level. Encourage each other as you pray for each other.

## WEEK 11

It is important in your discussion this week that you stay close to the idea of "deeper courage," rather than the simplistic, macho definition of courage. You might want to spend time discussing the difference before talking about the following questions.

- Discuss the people or situations in your life that make you feel like a "grasshopper." What do you do in those situations?
- Where do you find yourself "standing alone"? Describe to the group how that feels, as well as what steps you take to have courage.
- Have you ever "put out a fleece"? Did it help? What ways have you experienced God's encouragement and affirmation of what you are doing?
- Is it hard for you to wait in situations? Describe a situation where waiting added to your courage.
- How do you struggle with maintaining the spiritual disciplines in your life? Which are harder for you? Do you struggle more with consistency or intensity?
- How does God's value system shape your life and give you purpose? In what ways can you improve?

Take time for each man to relate what he has been learning about himself this week. Then ask for specific ways you can pray for each other throughout the coming week.

## WEEK 12

As you discuss the questions this week, try to stay focused on the concept of truthfulness as being more than fact. Focus on how it includes the knowledge of different realities as well. If this understanding is not clear, take the time to discuss it together so that you are in agreement with your basic understanding and definition.

- If truth is more than an accurate fact, how would you define it? In thinking of that definition, apply it to Jesus' statement that He is the truth.
- In what ways have you experienced the truth of the spiritual realities? What would you see differently in your life today if Elisha prayed for you that your eyes would be open to see God?
- What are some of your fears or reservations about accepting different aspects of spiritual reality?
- Have you ever tried to help God out? What were the consequences? How did God ultimately act in those situations?
- What are some of your doubts? How comfortable are you in discussing honest doubts? It's important as you discuss this question that you don't try to answer another person's doubt with proofs that work for you. You can share how you have handled your own doubts.
- In what ways do you feel your own integrity is being challenged today? How can the group help you with this?

Take the time needed for everyone to talk. Then share prayer requests and, if everyone is comfortable, pray for each other. Or you can simply commit to pray for each other through the week.

## WEEK 13

It is easy to feel judged in a discussion of responsibility. Be careful to avoid this as you discuss these questions. Try to keep it in the context of positive steps you can each take to continue moving in the right direction. If you are feeling as if the discussion is becoming judgmental, speak up and let the others know how you feel.

- Describe ways you believe you act responsibly. How good are you at sizing up a situation, seeing what needs to be done, and then doing it?
- Describe a situation in which your passivity led you to react irresponsibly. How do you "own" your irresponsibility?
- What is your understanding of what Paul calls the "weaker brother"?
- Is there a situation in your life now in which you have to take into consideration this weaker brother? Describe it.
- Shifting blame is a common response. In what kind of situations are you most likely to want to shift blame? How do others react when you do this?
- What situation(s) did you identify within your family where you need to be more responsible (i.e., taking initiative and following through)? What first steps did you list? How are you doing?
- Where are you resisting responsibility in your life? Who is your "Wendy," who helps you continue to resist by being responsible for you?

As the weeks have progressed, your time together has probably become more open as you relate things to each other that are much more personal. Continue to do this, both in your talking and in your praying.

## WEEK 14

As you discuss the following questions, try to affirm the leadership abilities and traits you see in each other. Be open and honest about your needs, making certain that everyone has an opportunity to talk.

- Describe ways you have resisted being a leader. What were some of the reasons? Where are you resisting today?
- Discuss together how each of you rated yourself on the four points of leadership:
  1. Priorities
  2. Delegating
  3. Being connected to those you are leading
  4. Listening
- Talk about steps you can take to improve each area.
- Who demonstrates to you the qualities of a servant-leader? Discuss why you feel that way.
- In your family and church, where do you sacrifice for the sake of being a leader? In what areas do you lead from the armchair, and in what areas do you lead from a hands-on position?

- What is comfortable and uncomfortable for you in the area of spiritual leadership? Are you more comfortable with action than with prayer?
- What could you begin to do in your family and in your church to express greater spiritual leadership?

Take enough time to cover the important points for each of you, making certain that everyone has a chance to participate. Then pray specifically for the needs expressed by each man in your discussion together.

## WEEK 15

It would be easy to talk about taking risks in the context of the crazy things we have done as men. Think of it more in the context of Paul's life. He was able to face anything with courage and confidence because he knew he was where God wanted him. Use that as the definition for your discussion.

- Describe a situation where you "played it safe." What were you protecting?
- How willing are you to take risks? What are some of the big risks that you have taken and the ones you are avoiding?
- When have you risked because of your faith? What were the results? How did you handle the disappointment if the results were not what you had expected?
- How do you differentiate between unnecessary risks and those that are necessary? What motivates men to take unnecessary risks?
- Describe situations in which you have taken on a giant in your life. What were the results? What made that person or thing a giant to you? How did God help you in that situation?
- How comfortable are you with your death? Talk about some of the things you would do differently if you knew that today you would die.
- What have you committed to do differently as a result of what you have learned through this study and through the group of men you have been meeting with?

End this session together by talking about the last part of the last question. Write down each man's commitment and then agree to pray specifically for each other, that you will each experience God's power to keep that commitment.

## WEEK 16

This may be your last meeting together. Take some time to discuss the possibility of continuing to meet and perhaps using other men's books that are available as a basis for your discussion. Make certain you have time to discuss the following questions.

- Where in your life do you feel that you can't be a finisher? How is unforgiveness related to that feeling? Who needs to be forgiven?
- When in your life have things felt hopeless and you've wondered, *What's the point in trying?* Did you recover in that situation? Describe what happened.
- In what ways was your father a finisher? What example did he give you?

- How do you plan on staying alive on the inside for the rest of your life? What are some of the steps you plan to take to ensure that?
- Look back over the past seven weeks at the traits of godly masculinity. (They are listed in the last day's devotional.) Discuss how you rated yourself on each one.
- Describe the goals you have set for yourself to grow in each of these areas in the next six months.

Agree to pray for each other, especially in regards to the goals you have shared. If you are not going to meet regularly, make plans to meet in six months so that you can talk together about how you have done with your goals.

# About the Author

**D**r. David Stoop is a clinical psychologist, clinical director of the Minirth Meier New Life Clinics, and co-host of the clinics' national radio broadcast. He is a graduate of Fuller Theological Seminary and received his Ph.D. from the University of Southern California.

*Jesus becomes all you need when you find out He is all you have!*